Hope House Way

Hope House Way

First published 2004
Researched and written by the Rotary Club of the Wrekin
Produced by Outcrop Publishing Services Ltd, Cumbria

Published by the Rotary Club of the Wrekin

ISBN 0 9548146 0 6

A CIP catalogue record for this book is available from the British Library.

Maps created by Mark Richards

Printed and bound in England by The Amadeus Press, Cleckheaton, West Yorkshire

Contents

Map Sections

Scale 1km
1 mile

About Hope House Children's Hospices

When a parent is told their child will not live to be an adult it is the start of an agonising journey. A childhood terminal illness challenges every belief, emotion and dream a parent may have for their special son or daughter.

Hope House has two hospices – Hope House in Oswestry and Ty Gobaith in North Wales. Our purpose is to support families facing the pain of losing a child. We offer practical and emotional help whenever and wherever it is needed.

It is about making the most of short and precious lives, enjoying the good days and sharing the bad ones.

The running costs of the hospices exceed £2 million each year. No charge is made to families for this service and we rely almost entirely upon voluntary donations.

We are delighted to have the support of Rotary International and are proud to be associated with this excellent project.

Ynglyn â Hosbisis Plant Hope House

Pan mae rhiant yn darganfod na wnaiff eu plentyn dyfu i fyny i fod yn oedolyn mae'n ddechrád o siwrnai boenus. Mae salwch angeuol mewn plentyn yn corddi pob crêd, emosiwn a breuddwyd sydd gan riant tuag at eu mab neu ferch arbennig.

Mae gan Hope House ddwy hosbis – Hope House yng Nghroesoswallt a Thŷ Gobaith yn Ngogledd Cymru. Ein pwrpas yw i gefnogi teuluoedd sy'n wynebu'r boen o golli plentyn. Yr ydym yn cynnig help ymarferol ac emosiynnol, pryd bynnag a ble bynnag y mae ei angen.

Rydym hefyd yma i wneud yn fawr o fywydau byr ac arbennig, mwynhau'r dyddiau da a rhannu'r rhai drwg.

Yn flynyddol, mae'r gôst o redeg y ddwy hosbis ymhell dros £2 filiwn. Does dim tâl yn cael ei godi ar y teuluoedd am ddefnyddio ein gwasanaeth ac yr ydym fwy neu lai, yn ddibynnol ar gyfraniadau gwirfoddol.

Yr ydym wrth ein boddau o'r gefnogaeth gan Rotary International ac yn falch o gael bod yn rhan o'r cynllun gwych yma.

Foreword/Rhagair

Welcome to this new long-distance walk, one of the longest and most picturesque in the United Kingdom. Planning for the walk started in 1998 when three members of the Rotary Club of the Wrekin in Wellington, Shropshire, had the vision for a new walk to celebrate the Millennium. Indeed the original title for the walk was the 'Wrekin Millennium Way'. Delays caused by Foot and Mouth and the magnitude of work associated with the creation of a walk of 539km (335 miles), together with the required funding, meant that final completion was not possible until 2004. At the same time, the name of the walk was changed to 'Hope House Way' not only to reflect that all the funds from the sale of this guidebook are being donated to Hope House but also to give publicity to the wonderful work performed by this children's respite hospice. By purchasing this guidebook you are contributing to the funding of the hospice, and by participating in the walk you are helping to boost the local rural economies. Whether you are undertaking the whole walk at one go, or just sampling the smallest of sections, I really hope that you enjoy the diversity of the terrain and the beauty of the scenery.

Croeso i'r daith gerdded hir yma, un o'r hiraf a mwyaf godidog yn y Deyrnas Unedig. Dechrewyd ar y gwaith o gynllunio'r daith ym 1998 pan gafodd tri aelod o Glwb Rotari Wrekin yn Wellington, Sir Amwythig, y weledigaeth o daith gerdded newydd i ddathlu'r Mileniwm. Yn wir, teitl gwreiddiol y daith oedd y "Wrekin Millenium Way". Gohuriwyd y Daith oherwydd clwy'r Traed a'r Genau, maint y gwaith ar drefnu creadigaeth taith gerdded 335 o filltiroedd, ynghyd a'r cyllid angenrheidiol a oedd ei angen, nid oedd yn bosibl cwblhau'r trefniadau cyn 2004. Ar yr un amser, newidwyd enw'r daith i "Hope House Way" nid yn unig i adlewyrchu y buasai'r arian i gyd o werthiant yr Arweinlyfr hwn yn cael eu gyfrannu i Hope House ond hefyd yn rhoddi cyhoeddusrwydd drwy'r llyfr hwn i'r gwaith bendigedig a wneir gan yr Hosbis Seibiant yma i Blant. Drwy brynnu'r Arweinlyfr yma, rydych yn cyfrannu tuag at gynnal yr Hosbis, ac drwy gymeryd rhan yn y Daith yr ydych yn cefnogi i hybu'r economi leol wledig. Os yr ydych yn unai ymgymeryd a'r Daith yn ei chyfanrwydd, neu grwydro ychydig o'r Adrannau, gobeithiaf yn fawr y gwnewch fwynhau amrywiaeth y tiroedd a phrydferthwch y golygfeydd.

C. Bonington.

Sir Chris Bonington CBE

Introduction

Hope House Way is a circular walk from the historic market town of Wellington in Shropshire. It is a walk, or if you prefer a series of walks, which offers a broad and diverse opportunity to all. It is varied in terrain and rich in history. The walk uses a combination of established paths, parts of other long and shorter well known routes, linked together by less well known, and little used, tracks, byways and footpaths.

The walk begins with an ascent of the Wrekin which, although a modest 407m, seems much higher because of its splendid isolation. From the top on a clear day, many of the features and high points of Hope House Way can be picked out. Soon after leaving this first of many tops ahead, the walk leads to Ironbridge, a World Heritage Site; then on to Wenlock Edge and the Clee Hills to reach Ludlow.

Much of the subsequent way is in mid Wales. From near Presteigne the route coincides with the Offa's Dyke Path National Trail through Kington to reach Hay-on-Wye. From here beautiful riverside walking lies ahead following the Wye Valley Walk up to Rhayader. After winding through the Elan Valley and on to Devil's Bridge, the route encounters the wild terrain of Plynlimon to reach Machynlleth. From here it is a short hop into the Dysynni Valley and the most westerly point of the walk.

The next few sections are probably the most challenging. They take in the high mountain terrain of Cadair Idris and the Arans to Bala, and then continue on to Llangollen via the Berwyn Mountains. Offa's Dyke Path is soon picked up again through to Welshpool and on to Montgomery. The walk then heads back east into England over the Stiperstones, the Long Mynd and the Stretton Hills. The return to Wellington once more tops the Wrekin, this time from the west, before dropping into town. In these parts we have a toast 'to all friends around the Wrekin'. When you have completed Hope House Way, you will have met many friends, and certainly been 'all around the Wrekin'.

Walking in Safety

Some of the sections of this walk are physically quite demanding, others are less so and require little experience of walking in the countryside. You should ensure you have the requisite skill and fitness before tackling a particular section. There are guidance notes on the grade of the section in the introductory information panel which precedes each section. The maps are drawn at a scale that is intended to help you follow the route on the relevant Ordnance Survey Explorer map. You should not try and rely on the information provided in this guidebook alone to navigate.

Whilst researching this walk we have tried to keep the risks to which you may be exposed to a minimum. But walking in the countryside can never be considered completely risk-free. Consider the following points and you will find your experience is both safer and more enjoyable.

• Occasionally the route is by, or crosses, busy roads. Take care here and remember that traffic is a danger even if you are on a minor country lane.

• Walk carefully in upland terrain, where the consequences of a slip can be very serious.

• Take care around agricultural machinery and livestock, especially if you have children or dogs with you.

• Consider the consequences of changes in the weather. Check the forecast before you set out and ensure you are carrying adequate and appropriate clothing. Remember the weather conditions can change very quickly at any time of the year and, in upland areas, mist and fog can make finding your way a lot harder. If you aren't confident about your navigation skills in poor visibility, don't set out in these conditions. In the summer months remember to take account of the heat and sun. Wear a hat and make sure you are carrying spare water. In winter it is prudent to carry spare clothing and a torch.

• Much of this walk will take you away from centres of population. Carry a whistle and a survival bag and bear in mind that mobile phone reception will often be non-existent. If you do have an accident requiring the emergency services, make a note of your position as accurately as possible and call 999.

Route Map

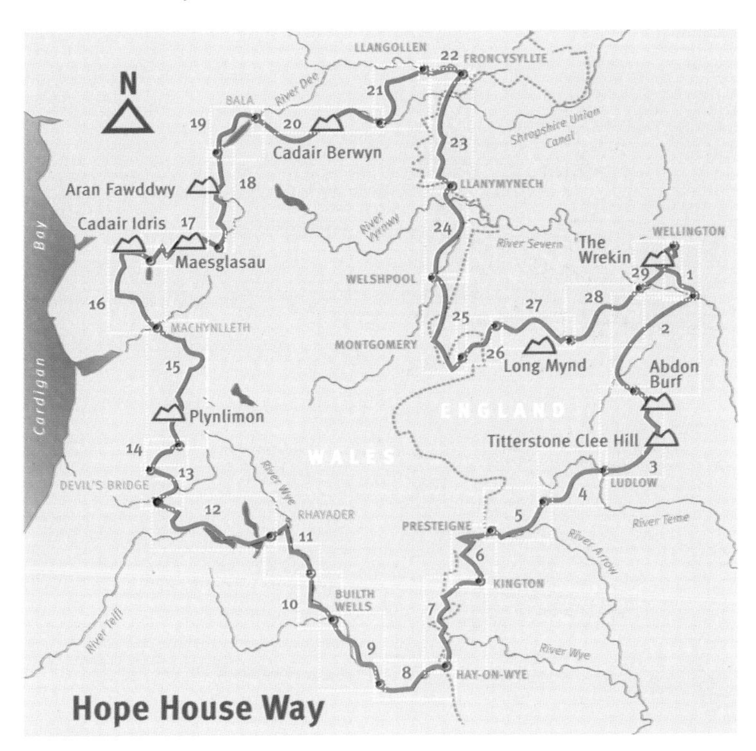

The Wrekin

Section 1
Wellington to Little Wenlock

Distance:	10km (6¼ miles)
Grade:	Easy
Terrain:	Metalled roads, woodland paths, tracks and footpaths, ascent of the Wrekin (407m). The route partly follows the Shropshire Way
OS Map:	OS Explorer 242: Telford, Ironbridge and the Wrekin
Route Map:	Map 1; Page 12
Guide Time:	3 hours

From the Community Clock in Market Square ❶ head S along Crown Street and continue in the same direction up Tan Bank. Cross directly over the ring road (with care!), continuing on what is still Tan Bank. Look out for a waymarked passage (Hutchison Way) on your right, approximately 50m

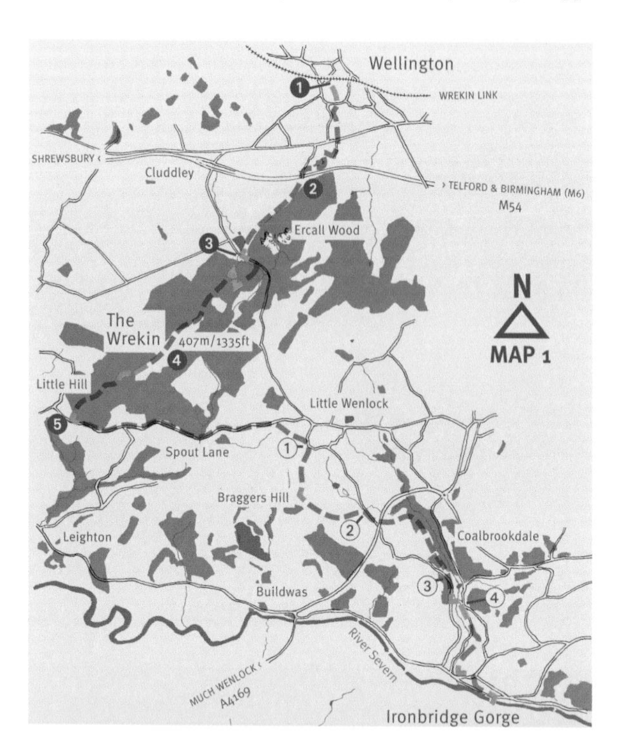

from the ring road. Follow this brick paviour passage and cross over Roseway into a further passage section, eventually emerging at the Holyhead Road. Cross directly over into Golf Links Lane and take the first turning on the right into Christine Avenue. After 200m take the public footpath on your left between the houses. This footpath leads up to the motorway boundary, where you branch right to follow a parallel line with the northern side of the M54 until reaching Ercall Lane ❷. Turn left here, crossing the bridge over the M54, and enter the Ercall Wood Nature Reserve. Follow the waymarked woodland path, which skirts the edge of Ercall Lane. Eventually you are forced back onto the highway, opposite the Buckatree Hall Hotel. Continue in the same direction along the lane until the road junction marked to Shrewsbury, at the end of Cluddley Reservoir ❸. Turn right here, then immediately left, through a gateway to begin the steady climb up the broad track to the top of the Wrekin.

The start of Hope House Way

After 800m keep on the main track as it almost hairpins to the right to pass Wrekin Cottage (locally referred to as Halfway House; refreshments available). The track twists and turns a little but continues to rise steadily through Hell Gate and Heaven Gate to reach the trig point and topograph at 407m ❹. On reaching the summit, continue on the same heading through the wooded 'log slide' on a steep descent, over a junction with the track that runs around the base of the hill, and into the dip between the Wrekin and Little Hill. Continue over several cross paths through mixed woodland to meet a wooden barred gate next to a stile to join Spout Lane at GR SJ614071 ❺.

Turn left towards Little Wenlock heading E along Spout Lane for approximately 2½ kilometres, passing a scout camp entrance on the left and continuing down a dip passing Spring Cottage. After passing Severnvale House on the left, watch carefully for a hidden signpost in an opening on the right, immediately beyond the junction with Leighton Lane (GR SJ642071). Enter a field with a hedge on the left, heading SE, cross a waymarked stile and keep following the hedge which deviates right then left to cross a stile at the field corner. Proceed up over the next small field to a stile opposite on a crest. Enter a grassy track with a high hedge on the left and a short sparse hedge to the right. The track then joins Witchwell Lane. Bear left towards a white cottage on the right with St Lawrence's Church beyond.

Wellington

Wellington appears to have a history going back at least 1,400 years but written records do not go back that far. The *Oxford Dictionary of Place Names*, suggests that it was originally known as 'Weo-leah-ingaton'. Translated to modern English this means 'the settlement by the temple in the grove'. So where was the temple in the grove? The most likely place is All Saints Church – or to be more precise – the lawn in front of it, where the old church stood. It was severely damaged during the Civil War and the 'new' church was built to replace it in 1790.

A market developed in the town and was confirmed by Henry III's charter in 1244, with a new market square and shopping streets being laid out. The market was moved from the Square in Victorian times and a new company subsequently purchased the charter rights from the lord of the manor and built a hall in Market Street. Nowadays the market days are Tuesday, Thursday, Friday and Saturday; there are also stalls outside the Victorian Hall.

In 1849 the railway came and Wellington became an important junction, with lines to Shrewsbury, Crewe, Stafford, Wolverhampton and to South Wales via Much Wenlock.

Although Wellington is on the edge of the East Shropshire coalfield, it is surrounded on three sides by fertile farmland, and became the area's chief livestock and wool market. It also developed into the local shopping, banking, professional, transport and trading centre. Now part of the thriving new town of Telford, Wellington retains most of its historic character and provides a worthy starting and finishing point for the Hope House Way.

Section 2
Little Wenlock to Ironbridge

Distance:	6km (3¾ miles)
Grade:	Easy
Terrain:	Metalled roads, footpaths and tracks, substantially following the Shropshire Way
OS Map:	OS Explorer 242: Telford, Ironbridge and the Wrekin
Route Map:	Map 1; Page 12
Guide Time:	2 hours

From the end of Witchwell Lane (facing St Lawrence's Church) (1) turn right into Church Lane. After 100m turn right into Buildwas Lane. Follow the lane for approximately 750m to the end of the metalled section and take a waymarked public footpath over a stile into a field on your left. (Note: This short section over Braggers Hill is a new footpath diversion.) Cross the field with the fence on your left to reach a further stile located between two communication masts. Cross the stile and head E across the field. At a further stile adjacent to a metal gate, cross into the lane/track at GR SJ653058 and turn left. After 300m the lane reaches Coalbrookdale Road (2).

Turn right, cross the bridge over the A4169 and turn immediately left to follow the metalled drive which leads past a waymarker to Leasows Farm. Immediately before the farm go through the metal gate on the right into the field. Cross the field heading diagonally E to a stile opposite and enter Lyde Brook Dingle. Follow the path into secluded woodland, down over a stile close by and then fork right at a marker down the hill. The path continues near the base of the dingle and then down a wooden stepped path across the stream. This is the locally popular Rope Walk.

Continue on the same path for 750m and emerge onto Darby Road (3). Turn down to the left passing the Quaker burial ground. Turn right immediately before the railway arches, and left at the end, under the arch before Coach Road. Continue past the Museum of Iron and right, up the incline, to join Dale Road. Turn right and continue straight down the road through Coalbrookdale. Cross the road to the left at the youth hostel and walk up Paradise. After 80m take the steep, metalled lane (marked footpath) immediately past a house and garages. Cross over the T junction at the top and follow the path diagonally opposite right, with an ivy-clad wall on the right, leading uphill via wooden steps to Lincoln Hill ④.

Continue over the cross track to the waymarked Rotunda, following the rising track to the right. From the Rotunda, take the wooden steps to the right and proceed steeply downhill. Turn right then left down further steps, then left to a path marked Lincoln Hill Road. Follow the path to a hardcore track leading to Lincoln Hill Road. Turn left up a steep road and, after approximately 260m, watch carefully on the right for a descending path in an opening with a low stone wall on the right. At the bottom of this path turn right then left down the Wharfage Steps. At the bottom of the steps turn left to walk along The Wharfage to the famous Iron Bridge.

Ironbridge

Once described as 'the most extraordinary district in the world', the Ironbridge Gorge is still a remarkable and beautiful place to visit. A huge amount of early industrial traces survive as furnaces, factories, workshops, canals and the settlements of Coalbrookdale, Ironbridge, Jackfield and Coalport. Today the Ironbridge Gorge is protected as a World Heritage Site and the remains of those important industries, complete with their relevant machinery, are preserved by the Ironbridge Gorge Museum Trust. There are nine main museums spread over an area of 9.6 sq km (6 sq miles) and it's impossible to do justice to them all in a single day. You can see the products that set industry on its path and the machines that made them. Watch and talk to the museum's craftspeople and costumed demonstrators as they work iron, fashion china and glass and bring alive the people who lived and worked here.

There are large Sites of Special Scientific Interest at Benthall Edge and Lincoln Hill, where rich plant and animal life flourishes. The much-revived River Severn is home to salmon, otter and kingfishers. Woodland walks weave along the valley, following old mining tracks, footpaths and the abandoned railway lines. The steep sides of the Gorge have never lost their fine woods. Some are genuinely ancient, others naturally re-colonised from pit mounds and spoil heaps or old plantations

The Ironbridge Gorge Museum Trust has a comprehensive website at www.ironbridge.org.uk.

Section 3
Ironbridge to Much Wenlock

Distance:	7.7km (4¾ miles)
Grade:	Easy
Terrain:	Ascent of Benthall Edge, footpaths, tracks and quiet lanes
OS Map:	OS Explorer 242: Telford, Ironbridge and the Wrekin
Route Map:	Map 2; Page 18
Guide Time:	2½ hours

Cross the Iron Bridge ❶ opposite the Tontine Hotel. Turn right following a Shropshire Way sign on the line of the former railway track, parallel with the River Severn.

At the end of the track, under the cooling towers of Ironbridge power station, cross the stile to the left and go initially left up the marked path, turning right at the junction on the rising traverse path waymarked Benthall. At a junction with tracks, continue straight ahead (SW), taking the ascending minor path to a stile with The Vineyards paddock area ahead. Cross the field, keeping the fenced hedge on your right, and two further stiles to reach Cowslip Cottage. Continue left of the cottage along the hardcore track up to a junction with Wyke Lane ❷.

Turn right and go along the lane to take the right fork past Manor Farm on the left. At the bottom of a descending right-hand bend, turn acutely left at a marker post (GR SJ641025).

Follow the track into Acklands Coppice and continue up the rising track passing Woodhouse Farm. At the end of the track enter a field over the stile. Keep close to the hedge on the right and continue to the corner of the field, ignoring a waymarked gateway on the right. (Note: At this point the definitive path, which heads off across the field is best avoided.) Continue to the field corner and follow round to the left.

Approximately 280m from the corner, take great care to locate a small marker and turn right through the overgrown hedge,

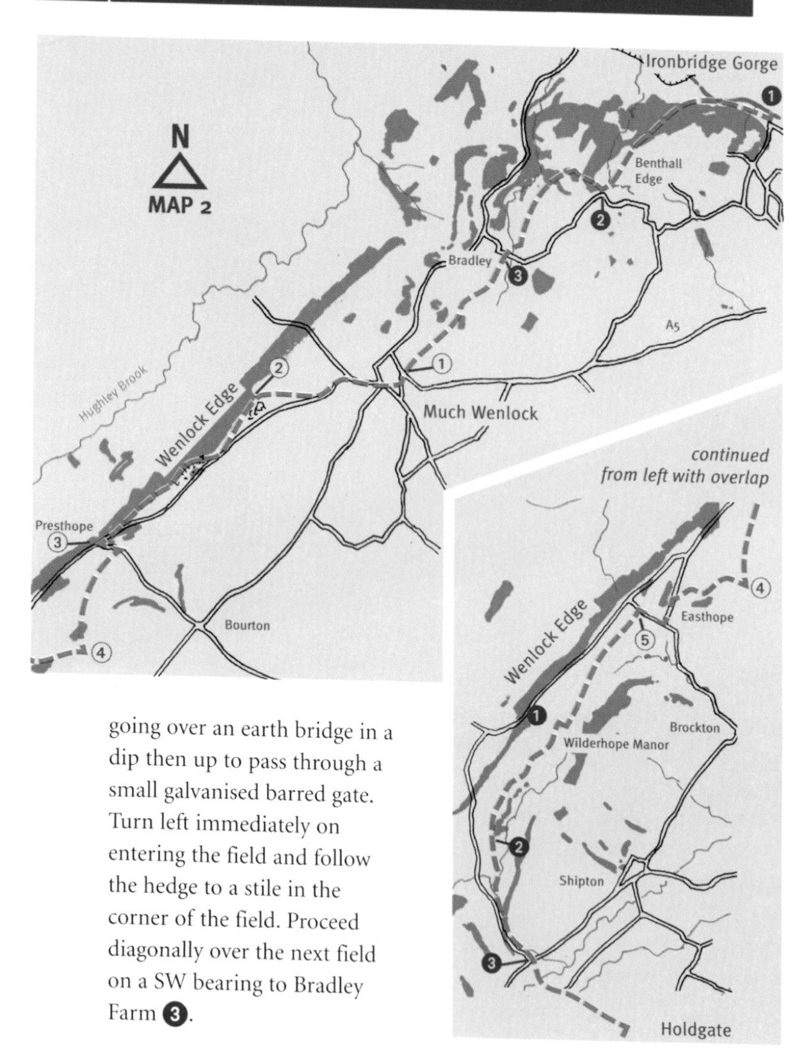

going over an earth bridge in a dip then up to pass through a small galvanised barred gate. Turn left immediately on entering the field and follow the hedge to a stile in the corner of the field. Proceed diagonally over the next field on a SW bearing to Bradley Farm ❸.

Cross two stiles, then pass between farm buildings to emerge on a road. Cross over and continue straight through the barred gate along a hedged track heading SSW to Downs Mill. Take the drive opposite and continue to reach Wenlock Priory. Proceed with a stone wall on the left (and car park on right) into Much Wenlock.

Section 4
Much Wenlock to Wilderhope Manor

Distance:	12.7km (7¾ miles)
Grade:	Easy
Terrain:	Lanes, tracks and footpaths
OS Map:	OS Explorer 217: The Long Mynd and Wenlock Edge
Route Map:	Map 2: Page 18
Guide Time:	3½ hours

Proceed along High Street (1) on the right-hand pavement of the A458 Shrewsbury Road, past Old Smithy Cottage on the right. At the Wenlock Edge sign on the right take the left turn towards Wenlock Edge and Church Stretton on the B4371, turning right, where signposted, to Blakeway Hollow. Continue as the lane becomes a rising track towards Blakeway Coppice. Bear left at a Wenlock Edge National Trust sign (2) towards Presthope. Continue for 3km. At the fork in the path go right and continue to a marker post on the left ('Presthope ¾ mile') by ascending steps. At a waymarked fork in the track go straight ahead and then left up a rising return to the crest and through a wooden gate to the car park, with Lower Hill Farm below on the right. Turn right onto the B4371 and proceed past the descending turn to Hughley and Church Preen on the right (3).

Turn left down the signposted road to Bourton. Opposite the entrance to a timber yard on the left go right along a poor metalled track heading SW. Follow the track between a shed on the left and an old quarry, right, and enter a hedged grassy track. Pass through a gate into a field with a hedge on the right for approximately 70m.

Leaving the hedge head S across a field past a small copse on the left and, further ahead, a single tree. Continue for 100m to cross the stile into a small copse by a waymarker. Follow the hedged, overgrown track over a further stile into a more open grass track, passing fields to the right and left. On entering a field keep to the hedge on the right past two old oak trees, then go up the field to a waymark post by Dove Plantation to the left. Continue S up over a stile into a field with a hedge on the right. Continue to a stile at the crest, cross and enter a further overgrown track heading down a tree-lined slope, bearing NW.

On reaching a field over a stile (4), follow the fence on the right and, at a fence corner, head across the field bearing SW to a marker post at the right-hand edge of an inclined copse (Natal Coppice).

Continue bearing right, by a telegraph pole, to cross a stile next to a gate and bear left. Follow the field hedge on the left to the top corner. Head WSW along the track at the far corner below a ridge through a gate. Go left on reaching the road and down into Easthope. By Manor Farm turn right along the road to Longville and Church Stretton.

On the outskirts of Easthope, and with Easthope Wood ahead at the crest, turn left beyond Easthope Cottage Farm (5) onto a waymarked track. Continue with Lutwyche Hall ahead past a house on the left to a stile on the right. Enter the field and proceed straight, then veer right on a grass track to a grassy bank to the right of saplings, and follow the fence line. Cross a stile on the right, just beyond a barn. Turn left through a farmyard, along a track with Lutwyche Hall to the right behind a raised beech hedge.

Continue along the track as it enters a field and turn right just past Pilgrim Cottage. Turn left after approximately 80m along a track with a hedge on the left. Continue to pass through wooden gates with Wilderhope Manor ahead.

Section 5
Wilderhope Manor to Holdgate

Distance:	4.4km (2¾ miles)
Grade:	Easy
Terrain:	Footpaths
OS Map:	OS Explorer 217: The Long Mynd and Wenlock Edge
Route Map:	Map 2; Page 18
Guide Time:	1 hour

Start from the track that skirts Wilderhope Manor ❶ to the right and continue through wooden gates with a red-brick building on the right.

Cross the stile into a field just beyond the Manor to the left of Wilderhope Farm buildings. Keep straight, crossing a narrowing field then along a track over a stile at the end. Follow a hedge on the right into a short, hedged, grassy track to enter a further field. Bear left by the hedge to the far right corner, then cross over a double-stiled wooden footbridge over a stream.

Turn left then right, following a hedge with a meandering stream on the left. Cross over to a stile near the field corner. Turn immediately left over a wooden stile/footbridge, re-crossing the stream. Turn right following a wire fence (Pudding Bag to the left and the Bog to the right). Pass Lower Stanway farm ❷ on the left, to a stile in the right corner, which leads onto a track.

Turn right then left over a stile into a field. Follow a marker to the left and, after crossing a bridge, turn right to follow the markers, keeping the stream on your right. The field eventually sweeps left with Brown Clee Hill dead ahead. On reaching a new, grey pebble-dash house turn right, over the brook, via a metal-railed bridge, then walk diagonally up and left on a SSE bearing to a stile in the hedge. Go left along the lane and up to a T-junction with the B4368 ❸.

Go right and across to a stile in the hedge (waymarked), keep close to the descending hedge on the left, leaving it to cross a bridge over the brook. You will see a short waymarker post on the right-hand side. Follow the hedge with trees on the right and Holdgate Moor on the left. Cross a stile at the end, on the right, and continue straight to the corner of the second field, turning left with a hedge on your right. Shortly turn right through a gate at a waymarker and cross the lane and the stile opposite. Keep straight over a small field with a fence/hedge on the left to a gully amongst trees at the far end. Cross the stream via stepping-stones, up to a stile and proceed up the field with hedge/fence/trees on the right noting the church ahead and Brown Clee Hill on the skyline. Continue up the long field to a stile in the top right corner and straight across the next rising field to the right of the church on the crest. At a metal gate, turn right onto a metalled road in the hamlet of Holdgate.

Colourful Shropshire woodlands

Section 6
Holdgate to Ludlow

Distance:	26.5km (16½ miles)
Grade:	Moderate/tough
Terrain:	Footpaths, quiet lanes, metalled roads, rough grassland, bridleways, numerous stiles/gates and steep ascents of Brown Clee and Titterstone Clee hills. (Reasonable skill with map and compass required, particularly in bad weather)
OS Map:	OS Explorers 217: The Long Mynd and Wenlock Edge and 203: Ludlow
Route Map:	Map 3; Page 24
Guide Time:	9 hours

Leave Holdgate ❶ by the lane with the church on the right. Passing a bungalow and farm buildings on the left and a post box in the wall on the right, turn left at a marker 40m further on. Go through the gate/stile with a barn on the right and, down the field, diagonally right to a gate. Proceed over the next field to a stile in the far right corner, continuing along a track between a hedge and trees, to the left of a further field.

Follow the track down to a wooden footbridge/stile over the stream and continue straight with a hedge on the left. Go uphill past a white timbered building on the right (Blue Hall). Cross the stile adjacent (opposite Blue Hall) on the left into a field. Turn right but leave the right-hand outstanding corner to go uphill to the gate opposite. Continue up and straight over the grass field, bearing slightly left to a stile then climbing over the steep fern bank (Mittons Rough ❷).

Bear left to a stile over a wire fence and go left up a track to a gate, then turn right to another gate. Continue straight on up, with a hedge on the right, to a gate at the top right corner into a hedged track. Follow this as it passes to the left of the red sandstone Earnstrey Hall and its buildings.

Brown Clee Hill now looms ahead. Follow the track down and up over a stream to a lane. Cross the stile opposite and go over a small field to a wooden stile/footbridge over the ditch. Follow the hedge/trees on the right over the next field to

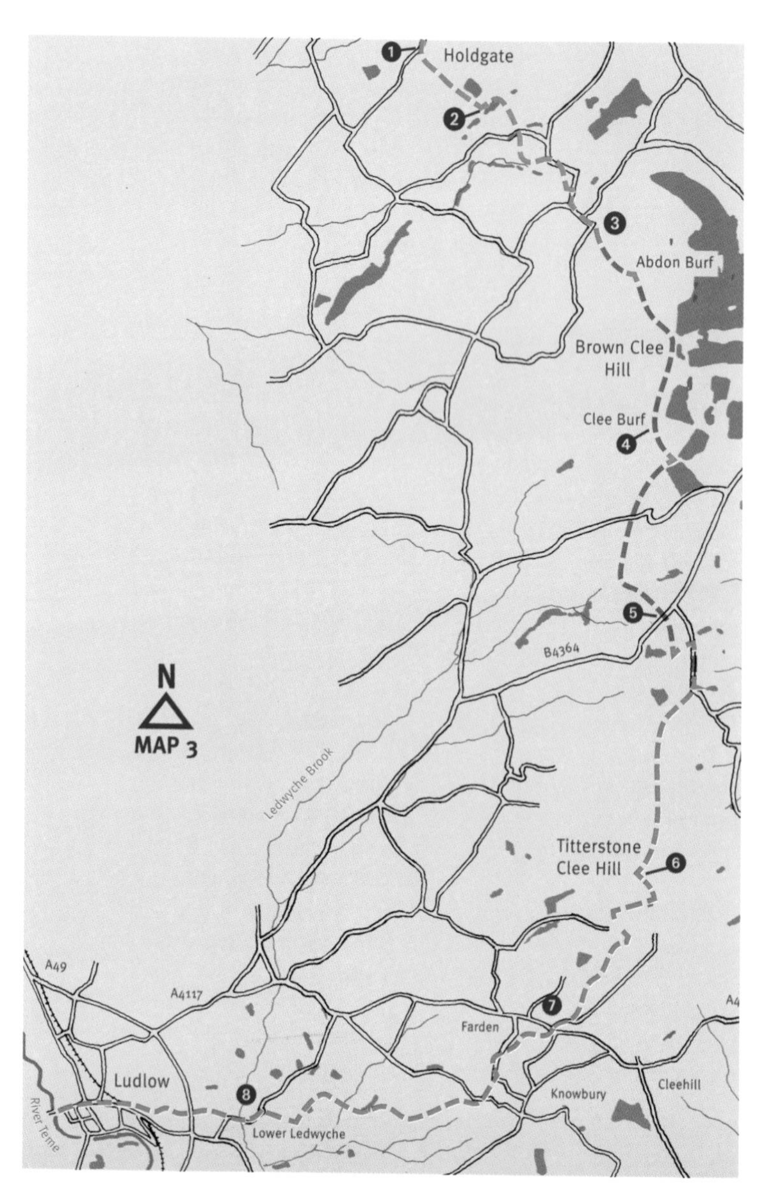

another wooden footbridge and stile in the far right corner, then turn left keeping to the hedge with Brown Clee ahead. Pass through a gate in the left corner and keep to the hedge/trees until reaching New Earnstrey Park farm buildings on the left. At the top left corner of the field go over a stile, turn left to a metalled road and turn right past Park View bungalow on the left. Watch closely for a stile by a gate in the dip to the right leading down to a muddy track with fence/trees to the right and sparse trees to the left.

Go down to a railed footbridge over the stream in a dip and up past a tree-lined gully on the left (Upper Earnstrey Park). Follow the hedge on the right, with a red-brick, stone edged building over to the left. At the field corner follow the right fence to a stile into a lane. Turn right along the lane and continue to a T-junction. Turn left towards Ditton Priors, go up the road and turn right by the red phone box (towards Cockshutford). Turn left just before the brow, past Bank House on the right, and cross the stile next to a gate to proceed up the Abdon Liberty sunken track ❸.

Go up the steep rise to Abdon Burf, the summit of Brown Clee. If you do not wish to visit the trig point and radio mast complex, turn right on reaching a line of concrete posts, towards Sandy Nap, keeping to the summit side of the posts.

From the summit, return to the concrete posts and continue as above. Keep close to the edge of a copse at first, then to a low wall/fence as you head S towards a pair of radio masts ❹. Soon you start to climb towards another peak. Continue up to the masts and pass through a gate to the left of the masts with Titterstone Clee straight ahead.

With care, note the path through moorland heading SSE. Do not follow the fence as it turns right. Descend on a moorland path and, as you approach a wood, bear right on the clearly defined path with the wood on your left. Continue down to a single wooden gate. Veer right into a downhill, tree-lined track on a WSW heading, soon reaching a waymarked post at GR SO592833, by a reservoir, with Upper Hill House immediately down on the left. Follow the grass path on the bank with trees to the right, not the track on the right. The bank falls away left.

Proceed downwards through an overgrown section with Mill Farm down on the left and Upper Bush on the right to a lane below Blackford. Cross straight over the lane and continue downhill with a phone box immediately on your right. This muddy track is waymarked and tree-lined, with fences to the right and left. It descends through Lower Bush with a tree-lined gully/stream on the left. Pass a building adjacent to the track on the left (Newton Cottage) and drop into the dip over a brook, ignoring the footbridge in the dip to the right.

Continue down and veer left with Newton Farm on the right, down a track into the dip and then up a tree lined track heading SSE passing the converted Coldgreen Barn, adjacent on the right, and the white Bromdon Cottage to the left on a crest.

Ascending Brown Clee Hill

At a T-junction with the B4364 (GR SO596815 ❺), with a red-brick house to the right on the corner, turn right and cross the road, going diagonally to the next waymark. Go through a metal gate and proceed up Dodshill Bank towards Knapp Farm. Follow the grassy track to a bend, with outbuildings on the left, and cross a stile on the right into a field. Go diagonally across to a dip with a stream, heading S. Cross a waymarked stile by a gate into a rising field. Keep right to a grit track and turn left passing a gate with a waymarker post. Follow the track NE to a road beyond a cattle grid. Turn right into a lane and proceed, with Titterstone ahead, towards Bromdon over the rise and into a dip. At GR SO601805 pass Upper Bromdon Farm before turning right along a stony lane (Callow Lane).

Continue as the track becomes a path and go through a gate towards Titterstone Clee. Head up S (eventually SW) to the summit and trig point, to the right of the radar masts and oversize golf balls ❻. Continue SE, skirt outside the wire fence of a quarry (taking great care if it is misty) and join a metalled track to continue past the radar dome on the left, and to the left of two further masts. At the end of the mast compound use the concrete path skirting the compound to the right. At the rear descend on a metalled track (cut out the bends), past the old quarry on the right. Leave the track at a hairpin bend after a metal gate, through a small gully, heading WSW, to join a track through more old workings. At the second concrete building (painted 'Outward Bound Croydon') veer left and descend the pulley incline gully, now grass covered, heading WSW. Continue down the incline for approximately 420m and, immediately after the concrete bridge, follow the short marker post on the left down a bank and along a grass track (SE), with a farm to the right. The grass track joins a hedge with trees on the right. Cross the metalled track and descend to a waymarked, railed wooden footbridge over Bensons Brook at Horseditch (GR SO590772).

Cross and turn right up a grassy path to a small wooden gate at the top of the rise. Enter a field, cross a small stream and follow the left perimeter up to

Nine Springs Farm, passing a white cottage on the left. Cross a stile then go up a track turning right after a metal gate. Continue WSW along the track over a stile to emerge onto a road. Turn right through Dhustone and follow the road to the junction with the A4117 ❼. Cross diagonally left to a waymarked drive, then go through a gate with a hedge on the left, towards the right of a stone building. Cross a stile down into a field and continue down, going over a stile by the white house opposite. Down the track turn left over a waymarked stile on the left in a hedge. Cross over a small paddock and a further stile down, to a muddy dip.

Go over a stream and then a stile on the bank, into an overgrown gully with a stream on the left. Proceed to a stile and up a bank into a small field. Go through a series of small fields via waymarked stiles to reach an open field with a bank to the right. Proceed S across to a church, leaving New House Farm down to the right, and cross the stile to the right of the graveyard, crossing a further stile to a road. Cross the lane and proceed through a gate into a field, with a wall and hedge on the left. Go straight ahead through a wooden gate in the next field, still with the hedge on the left. Continue through the next wooden gate and keep left to a hidden stile in the far left corner. Enter an overgrown track descending to a lane at GR SO569749. Turn right and then left at a right-hand bend in the lane at a waymarked stile and continue diagonally down over the field (WSW).

Find a stile in the opposite hedge into the next field, still heading WSW down to a double stile towards the far right corner, to the right of a gate. Continue over a ditch and keep the hedge on the left, with the stream in the ditch alongside. Turn right at the far left corner to a gap in the hedge on the left. Pass through the gap and along the track down a field with Ludlow ahead and to the right. Take the waymarked path opposite and turn right, ignoring the leftward waymark. Follow the hedge on the left down a track heading WNW, then NW, past a waymarked post to a gate, with a further waymarker post on the right. Turn here and head diagonally left across fields, leaving at an oak tree in the hedge on the left. Keep heading SW but turn right by a single oak tree to cross a bridge into the next field. Head for a gate and stile opposite. Follow the left-hand edge of the next field, then cross the ditch to follow the same heading. Continue to the next waymark and turn left to continue SSW with the hedge to the right, veering and skirting right of a wood and onto a track. Bear right at the end of the field corner to cross the wood then follow the clearly defined track, with a wood and a pool on the right, to emerge through a gate on the corner of Squirrel Lane in Lower Ledwyche ❽.

Turn left down the lane with woodland to the right. Go over a stone bridge where the lane crosses Ledwyche Brook. Continue along the lane, rising towards a high voltage pylon. Leave the lane at a left-hand bend, going straight ahead over a double stile. Proceed with the hedge on the left, passing a pylon and electricity sub-station to another double stile in the top left corner. Go up the next field to the top left corner and up the steps onto the bypass (A49) at GR SO528747. Cross the busy road carefully to a marker diagonally right. Descend to and cross a wooden footbridge and stile. Go ahead over waste ground to join the metalled cul-de-sac of a small industrial estate. Turn left then right to emerge onto a road. Cross to a marker post and turn right, then cross over Blashfield Road and, after approximately 40m, opposite a garage, turn left into a metalled path heading W through a new housing estate.

Cross the next road and a further road (Normandie Close) to emerge down to join Dark Lane. Turn right and continue with a view of Ludlow to the left. At the foot of the lane bear left and continue up through a housing estate, then straight on down the steep Rock Lane. Past Housman's Crescent on the left, take the next left turn through to a small metalled downhill path. Turn right, going under the railway to join Sheet Road, then turn right again and head for the church tower, passing the Bishop Mascal Centre on the left. Go up into Lower Galdeford and on into the centre of Ludlow.

Section 7
Ludlow to Wigmore

Distance:	12.9km (8 miles)
Grade:	Easy
Terrain:	Quiet lanes, footpaths, bridleway, open fields and steep woodland paths
OS Map:	OS Explorer 203: Ludlow
Route Map:	Map 4; Page 30
Guide Time:	3½ hours

From Ludlow Castle ❶ descend Dinham and cross Dinham Bridge to join the path on the left and ascend the steps. Follow the waymarked permissive route over Whitcliffe Common. On joining a road turn right to Lower Wood Road and ascend the waymarked permissive path on the left, keeping parallel with the road to the right. At a T-junction on the path turn left, emerging on a road opposite a Forestry

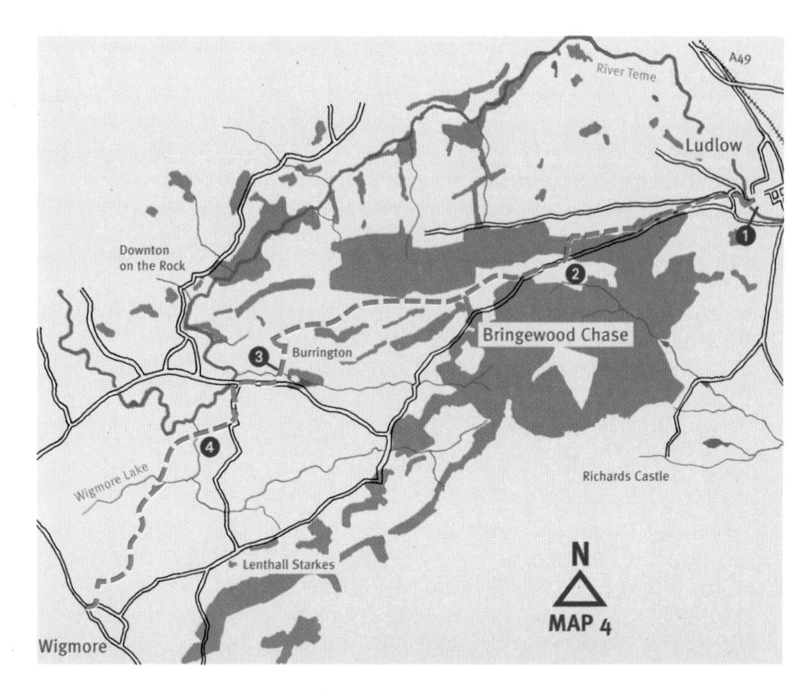

Ludlow

Ludlow has been described as one of the most beautiful and distinguished country towns in England. Originally, a Norman 'new town', it developed as an administrative centre and was the seat of the Lord President of the Marches until 1689. Lawyers and Royal Messengers bustled through the town; courts sat and fine Tudor houses such as the Feathers were built. Cloth manufacture and the sale of wool brought prosperity to the area.

Much of Ludlow's medieval street pattern survives almost intact, along with many ancient properties. Ludlow Castle is over 900 years old and features examples of architecture from the Norman, medieval and Tudor periods. In the 15th century, the castle became a royal residence housing, amongst others, the princes Edward and Richard, later murdered in the Tower of London. The 15th-century Church of St Laurence, one of the largest parish churches in the country, commemorates A E Housman, the author of *A Shropshire Lad*, in its churchyard.

Fashionable society in Georgian Shropshire built their fine brick houses in Broad Street and Mill Street, which remain today. Glove making became the main industry until the early 19th century.

Today Ludlow is a busy rural market town attracting visitors from all over the world. The Arts Festival held at the end of June features an open-air performance of a Shakespearean play in the castle. Much of the area around Ludlow is designated an Area of Outstanding Natural Beauty including the 'blue remembered hills' of A E Housman's *A Shropshire Lad*. Fine eating places, a museum and individual shops all help to make Ludlow a jewel in the Shropshire crown.

Commission sign. Turn right and follow the track along the edge of open, falling ground. At the first footpath junction turn left and ascend a path to the forestry road, cross it and continue ascending S to the road ❷.

Turn right along the road to Hazel Coppice and join the ascending forestry track on the right. At a junction follow a further waymarked path through a gate, descending towards Monstay Farm. Over a waymarked stile, cross the rising field, following the fence on the left, and head for a waymarked stile in the left-hand corner. Head WNW towards a wooded area and join a well defined track over a waymarked stile.

Follow the track on the side of the sloping wooded area heading W. After passing through a gate onto a stone track, head down (W) to New House Farm and beyond, descending past Burrington

Farm through a village. Turn right to the church ❸, go through the churchyard and past the porch to a stile in the corner. Crossing the stile, follow the fence on the left to a further waymarked stile, continuing through a meadow to another waymarked stile in a hedge. Follow, with the hedge on your left, to a stile past a duck pond. Continue in the same direction towards a bridge and locate a stile beside a gate on the left leading to a road. Take the road signposted to Leinthall Starkes.

At the first junction continue ahead to The Willows ❹ and along the stone track to a bridge over a stream and a waymarked stile beyond on the left. Cross the stile and head S following the stream on the left to a gate. Go through the gate and continue to follow the stream round the edge of the field past a pine plantation on the left and then follow the stream W towards another pine plantation.

Before reaching the second plantation go through a gate and, keeping the stream on the left, proceed to another gate. Go through the gate and over the bridge. Continue SSW across the field to a gate. Through the gate, continue SSW with a hedge and fence on the left to a waymarked gate in the corner of the field. Go through the gate and follow the stream on the right to a gate on the right. Cross the waymarked bridge on the right and immediately turn left to a waymarked stile after 20m.

Cross the stile and head SW to a stile in a fence. Over the stile, continue SW to a gate. Go through the gate and over a wooden bridge. Follow the hedge on the right, heading S to a wooden bridge on the right. Cross the bridge and turn left to a stile in a hedge. Cross the stile and ditch on a plank. Turn right and follow the edge of the field to the corner.

Continue over the waymarked wooden bridge and stile, turn left towards a caravan park and enter over a stile in the top right corner of the field. Proceed through the caravan park to reach Wigmore at the Compasses Hotel.

Section 8
Wigmore to Presteigne

Distance:	13.7km (8½ miles)
Grade:	Easy
Terrain:	Quiet lanes, footpaths, bridleway, busy road, woodland, open fields and riverside paths
OS Map:	OS Explorers 203: Ludlow and 201: Knighton and Presteigne
Route Map:	Map 5; Page 33
Guide Time:	3 hours

From the Compasses Hotel ❶ go uphill (W) to reach the A4110 then turn left to a telephone box. Continue right, up a waymarked road past a building onto a stone track. At the junction keep left, taking the waymarked footpath on the left before a metal gate. Ascend to a stile, turn left to a waymarked stile in the hedge on the left and head S, now descending to a stream and waymarked footbridge.

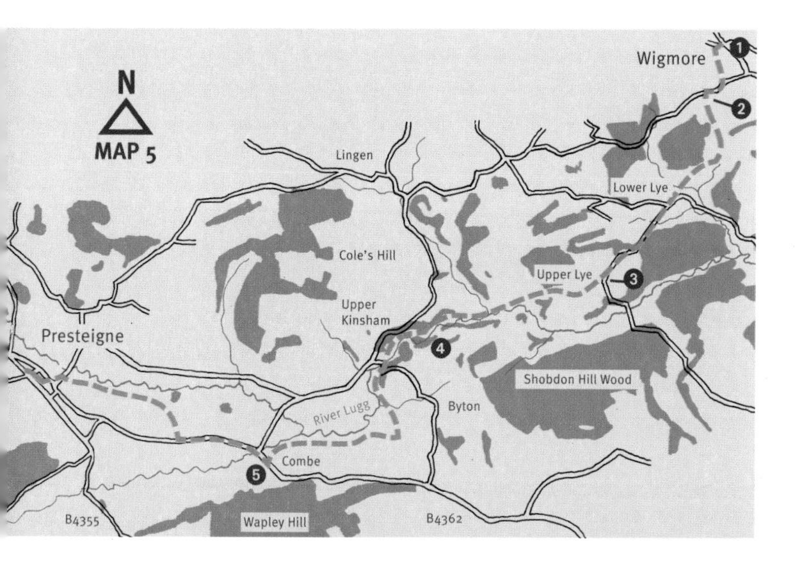

Turn left through a gully and head SW, ascending towards Barn Farm ❷ with a stile in the far right corner of an undulating field. Cross the stile to reach a metalled road, then turn right, to go left again opposite Barn Farm. Continue up the rising stone track. At the beginning of a wooded area and a bend in the track, cross to the waymarked stile on the left into a field and cross SE to the far corner. Follow the hedge on the left to Barnetts Barn and a waymarked metal gate.

Through the gate bear right on a track through a further gate heading S then, bearing SW, descend to Woodhampton House. Turn left down a stone road and, at a bend, take the waymarked footbridge on the left. Ascend the field (SW) to a stile in the hedge and onto a metalled road. Turn left through Lower Lye and, at the junction, take the road to the left to Upper Lye ❸.

Continue on the road (W) past Bach Brooke Farm to a steep downhill section. At the bottom of the hill turn right and immediately on the left, with a ford and bridge with a finger-post on the left, go over the bridge and follow the track to a gate. Through the gate turn immediately left, through a hedge into a meadow. Turn right (W) towards the river. Keeping the river on the left proceed to a gate. Go through the gate and bear left (SW) to a wooden gate. Go through the gate and cross a ditch to a second wooden gate. Continue WSW keeping the river on the left. Through a gate, enter a forest ❹.

Keeping the river on the left, follow the path to a wooden gate and then a second wooden gate onto a metalled road. Follow the road and, at a T-junction, turn left (S) and cross the bridge. Turn right (WSW) at a metal gate and follow the path through trees.

Keep to the waymarked track close to the river on the right, eventually bearing left, heading SE. Cross the waymarked stile and bear left over a wooden bridge to head up the bank on the left.

Proceed with the river on the right to the edge of a field and bear left to a waymarked wooden bridge. Cross the bridge and head S for a waymarked stile directly across the field opposite the bridge. Over a stile continue SSE with a fence on the right to a waymarked gate on the right. At the crossing of paths turn right, continue to a waymarked wooden footbridge over a stream and over a field to the bank of the River Lugg on the right. Keep alongside the river for 1.5km to join the road ❺, turning right towards Presteigne.

Continue over the bridge ignoring the right turn to Kinsham and Lingen. Follow the right-hand grass verge of the road for approximately 1km. Turn right onto a waymarked cement and grass track, past a timbered white cottage on the left. Follow the track to a gate with a stile into a field. Head WNW to a two-stile footbridge over a stream.

Proceed diagonally over the next field on a NW heading to a stile in the opposite corner by the river. Follow the riverbank on the right, past several markers and keep ahead (W) over a stile. Continue straight to another stile in the opposite hedge, 20m in from the right-hand corner.

Proceed over the next field and look for a stile 10m in from the opposite left-hand corner. At the end of this field cross a small footbridge. Keep to the left, heading towards the church, and continue over the next field to a stile and a further field with a stile on the left leading to a wire-fenced and hedged lane.

Pass three red-brick houses on the right and emerge along a small road bounded by further buildings to a T-junction. Turn left and continue left into Presteigne centre, past St Andrews Church immediately on the right. An alternative is to cross over from a T-junction into the gated churchyard with the church on the left. Past the church go acutely left on a path to the town centre. The attractive road passes the Judge's Lodging and the Shirehall and leads to an old restored and painted Co-op building at the Town Cross junction.

Presteigne

This border town is often claimed to be 'neither in Wales nor in England but simply in Radnorshire'. Set amongst the lovely countryside of the Marches, Presteigne was described by Lord Chief Justice Campbell in 1855 as 'a sort of paradise'. Little has changed since Campbell's time in this former county town, where one step over a tiny stone bridge takes you into England. The dramatic and wild mountains of mid Wales contrast with the rich lowlands of the border counties and make this thriving border town (Llanandras in Welsh) a perfect place to spend some time.

The town's riverside walk and nature reserve (the Withybeds and Wentes Meadow) are important locally for wildlife. There's also a lovely park on the site of the old castle (The Warden) and Silia Wood, an outstanding arboretum in which to stroll. On the edge of town, Bryan's Ground is worth a visit. It's a reconstructed Edwardian garden and home of the horticultural journal Hortus.

The former prominence of the town as the legal and administrative centre of Radnorshire (now part of Powys) are echoed in the Judge's Lodging. This is the town's outstanding tourist attraction, a stunningly restored Victorian town house with courtroom, cells and servants' quarters. Audio tours take you back to the gas-lit 1860s. The building also houses the tourist information centre, where you can pick up a copy of the town trail. The trail takes you on a trip into the past through the streets of this charming town. The notable buildings include the Duke's Arms, home to the last (and furthest travelling) mail coach in the UK; the Red House, home of Rear Admiral Puget, after whom Puget Sound on Vancouver Island is named; the Radnorshire Arms Hotel, a fine black and white building and one-time home of Sir Christopher Hatton (a favourite of Elizabeth I); and St Andrew's Church on Broad Street, architecturally renowned and housing a superb 16th-century Flemish tapestry. Newell's ironmongery shop, also in Broad Street, was established in 1770 and survived for over 200 years until 1974, when the Museum of Welsh Life purchased its extraordinary collection of over 3,000 stock items, many still in mint condition although dating from the 19th century.

On the hills above the town you will find the Powys County Observatory, where the wonders of the sky are presented to you through tours which include the planetarium and camera obscura. Local treasures include standing stones at Walton, holy wells at Pilleth, and the ruins of Stapleton Castle, which look down over the town. Several exhibitions are held at the side of the old Market Hall, and not for nothing is this town known as the 'Town of Festivals'. From the Quilt Festival to the Sheep Music Festival, there is usually something going on in this delightful bustling town.

Section 9
Presteigne to Kington

Distance:	15.3km (9½ miles)
Grade:	Easy/moderate
Terrain:	Roads, bridleways, tracks, byways and footpaths, some steep ascents and descents. The route follows, in part, Offa's Dyke Path National Trail
OS Map:	OS Explorer 201: Knighton and Presteigne
Route Map:	Map 6; Page 38
Guide Time:	4½ hours

From the Methodist church ❶ next to the Royal Oak pub, proceed up the slope to the main road. Cross it and enter Warden Road. Continue walking out of town for approximately 400m past Silia Cottage on the left and, 100m beyond, take the waymarked lane to the left ascending to Harley's Farm. Continue along the tree-lined track, through a gate (alternative footpath parallel) and along a green lane, ascending to the corner of Harley's Hill Wood.

Fork right (NW) at a waymark, crossing the open field with a farm on the right. Locate a stile to the right of a gate in front of the farm. Cross the stile and a field to a further stile beside farm buildings. Turn left and up a track, through a gate, ascending towards a small wood on the left. Continue along a gorse-hedged road past The Warren and Gumma Wood on your right, taking time to enjoy the beautiful rolling countryside at the summit.

Pass through a gate and continue along the tarmac road, passing through a second gate and a farmyard on the left. Continue to Middle Thorn Farm ❷ and a junction, then turn left with farm buildings and a house on the right. Continue along the ascending track (S) then descend towards a cottage, joining a metalled road. Continue walking straight on along the road, eventually descending, with hills and rolling countryside ahead and an old disused quarry on the right-hand side.

Look out for concrete steps with a wooden handrail on the left in the bank ❸. Take the steps to follow a waymarked track (the Offa's Dyke Path National Trail) into a field, with a telephone mast on the right. Follow the track close to the boundary fence and tree line.

Pass over a series of waymarked stiles with a boundary fence alternating to the right and left of the track. Descend, then ascend steps, go over a stile continuing in same direction, to further steps and on to a metalled road. Turn left and then right with Old Burfa House on the left. Continue past Old Burfa Farm and locate a waymarked track. Continue past a demolished stone building on the left, along a wooded track eventually joining a minor road.

Turn left towards the B4362 then right on reaching it and, continuing for approximately 400m, look out for a waymarked sign on the left at Lower Harpton Farm. Take the track to the left, with farm

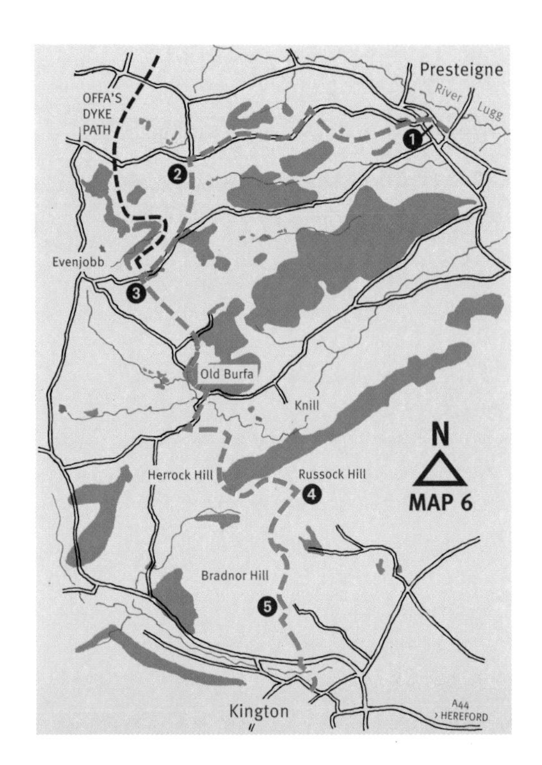

buildings on the right and, at the end of the building complex, leave the track and enter a field by a gate and stile on the right. Cross the small field diagonally, heading for a wicket gate through onto a green track. Turn left and follow the ascending track past a cottage on the right. Proceed up the track with a fence and trees and with a slope down to the left.

Take the right-hand fork at a waymarker post on the ascending track and continue over a stile to the summit, following a further waymarker post to the right, along a clearly marked track. Head left at a small hawthorn tree then go further left (E) towards a gate and stile.

Crossing the stile, continue up the track past a marker post to a stile, keeping the fence to your left. At some sheep pens at the edge of a wood, bear right, keeping the fence to your left over a further stile to a waymarker post ❹. Turn right (SSW) across an open field, with a clear ridge indicating the path, to the fence opposite and locate a stile. Continue on the waymarked track towards a hedge on the left and descend to a waymarker post. Descend further, away from the hedge to a stile next to a gate. Over the stile, head left (SE) across a sloping field (note the small farm to your left) to the next stile located alongside a gate and oak tree. Continue to head SE across three sloping fields to a wood and, keeping the wood to your left and a fence to your right, head towards a gate and stile ahead. Cross the stile and a field towards the top right-hand corner, passing buildings (Quarry House) to your left. Pass through the gate onto a metalled road and turn right over the cattle grid onto Kington Golf Course ❺.

Locate the waymarker posts across the fairways (beware of flying golf balls!) heading S, descending with the clubhouse on your left and a cottage ahead. Head towards further dwellings (Bradnor Green) and locate a grassy right of way between them. Proceed on the descending narrow path to a field and continue across fields in the same direction, towards further buildings (Rhue Ville) to reach a metalled road. Go down the road to the Kington bypass and cross it, slightly left, towards a footbridge.

Section 10
Kington to Newchurch

Distance:	12.9km (8 miles)
Grade:	Moderate
Terrain:	Quiet lanes, footpaths and some steep hill walking, following Offa's Dyke Path National Trail
OS Map:	OS Explorer 201: Knighton and Presteigne
Route Map:	Map 7; Page 41
Guide Time:	3½ hours

After crossing Kington bypass ❶ locate a footbridge and cross into an ascending road (Crooked Well). Go straight on past a fingerpost and crossroads with Bradnor View Close, round a bend and towards the town centre. Proceed past St John's House on your right and into The Square, turning right at the Swan Hotel. Continue along a slightly ascending road passing a church on your right, then bear right at a small junction marked Hergest Croft. Continue for a short distance beyond the church, taking a left turn marked 'Ridgebourne/ Hergest Croft'. Continue on the ascending road, passing the tourist information centre on the right, heading W. Keep on this heading (W) for some distance after the tarmac surface ceases, through a farm gate and past a directional sign, indicating Hergest Ridge, into open rising country. This takes you away from the wooded area on the right to a waymarker post. Bear right still heading W. At a junction of footpaths ❷, continue on a WSW route, do not take the right fork but note the path joining from the left. Locate a waymark to the right of the path and continue, with a small plantation on your left. Maintain this heading to the next waymark, taking you W, and continue past the next junction of footpaths, again heading westward along Hergest Ridge.

The appropriate path is well waymarked and maintains a WSW heading. Bear left at a waymarker post at the junction of paths and, at the next fork, bear left and continue past more waymarks, descending on

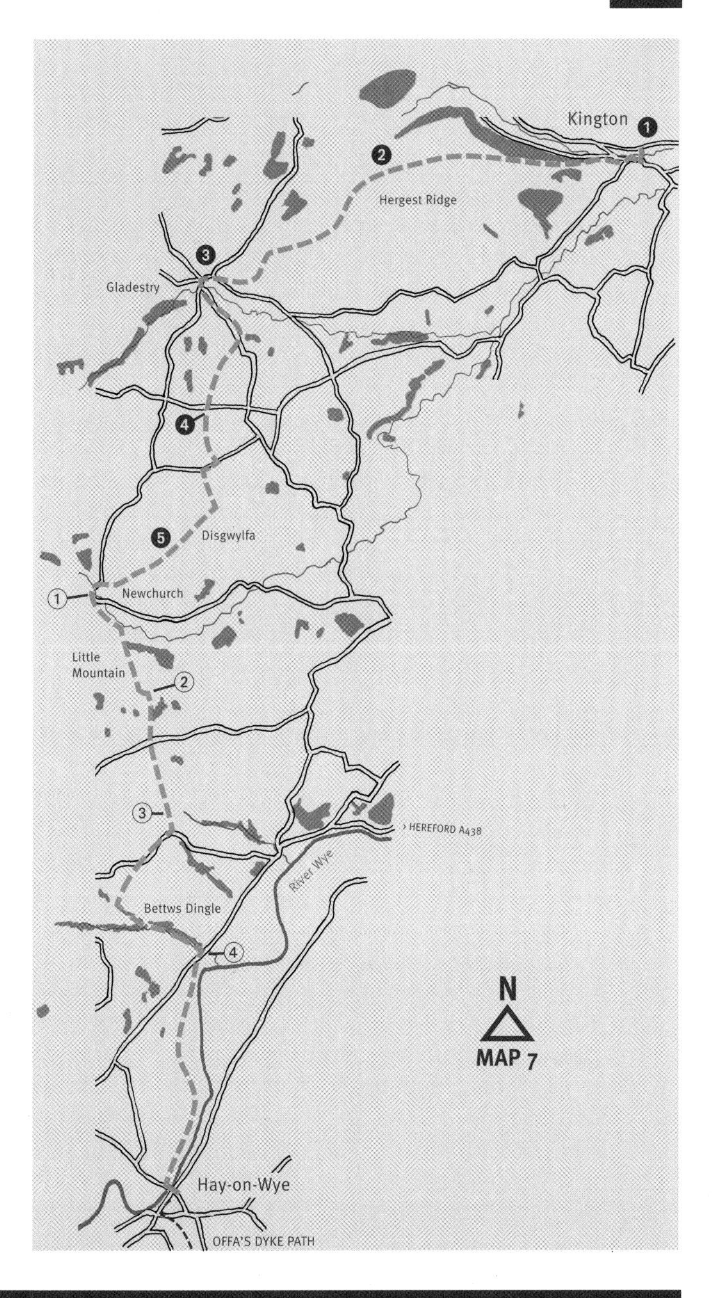
Kington
1
2
Hergest Ridge
3
Gladestry
4
5
Disgwylfa
1
Newchurch
Little
Mountain
2
3
> HEREFORD A438
River Wye
Bettws Dingle
4
N
MAP 7
Hay-on-Wye
OFFA'S DYKE PATH

a WSW bearing. Fork left at a further waymark and continue to descend towards a road and the village of Gladestry ❸. At a gate take the metalled road past a house on your left, pass through a further gate and continue to descend. Bear right at a junction towards a school, but at the next junction (before the school), bear left passing the post office on the right and the Royal Oak pub (left). At the next junction bear left, over the river bridge and immediately turn left up a road, passing Offa's Dyke Lodge. Continue on this road past a farmhouse and buildings, at which point leave the metalled road to continue straight on, following an Offa's Dyke waymark.

The path now ascends and crosses a stile, after which it turns right and ascends to a further waymark. Bear left and continue upwards to the next waymark at a junction. Head straight on, locating a finger-post on the right with the route passing through a tree-lined section bearing SSW. Ascend towards double gates with a waymarked stile, beyond which turn left, following a double fence and hedge to a further stile. Crossing, turn right, descending towards a stone building and stile. Over the stile proceed with Stonehouse Barn on the right and a beech/conifer hedge on the right to a waymarked gate. Join a road ❹, turn right and almost immediately left over a waymarked stile into a field with a fence and hedge on your right. Over further stiles continue towards a coppice and some farm buildings. After the next stile join a driveway, turning right towards Grove Farm and, just beyond, turn left down a lane marked 'No Through Road'. Pass a small farm with a house on the left and buildings on the right. Continue on down the lane to a stile and go left at the fork.

Locate a waymarker post and turn right up the path. Continue passing clear waymarks to a summit ❺, then descend on the same bearing. Fork right at the next junction to a waymark 200m ahead. Continue SW passing further waymarks. Note a gate on your left but maintain the same heading in the field with a fence and hedge on your left. Descend to a gate and enter a lane, through a small farmstead to the main road at Newchurch.

Section 11
Newchurch to Hay-on-Wye

Distance:	11.3km (7 miles)
Grade:	Easy
Terrain:	Quiet lanes, tracks and footpaths
OS Map:	OS Explorer 201: Knighton and Presteigne
Route Map:	Map 7; Page 41
Guide Time:	2½ hours

Head S on the B4594 from the telephone box (1) and take the left turn passing a church on the left following the signpost to Michaelchurch. At the next junction bear right, with farm buildings on the right, and continue along a tree-lined lane. After ascending to a waymarker post leave the metalled road and head straight on continuing upwards. Pass through a gate and follow the zig-zag path ascending to a stile and gate. Continue over and ascend to the next stile and gate with the path now levelling out to reach the next stile and gate. Continue in the same direction, always keeping the hedge on your left to join a further lane (Red Lane) (2), after crossing a stile in the top left-hand corner of a field and a further stile. Bear right along the lane to a T-junction. At this continue

Checking the route in the Wye Valley

straight across through a gate onto an ascending path with a stone wall on your right. Through a further gate begin to descend with a line of trees on the right to a gate and road.

Turn left to a house (Cae Higgin ③) and locate the stile immediately opposite on the right to enter a field, bearing left. Cross the stile in the next fence, continue over a field and further stile onto a road. Turn right, keeping on the main road ascending to a crossroads. Turn left as indicated by a fingerpost and, at the junction, continue straight on, descending to a road. Watch for a fingerpost and steps on the left in a wooded area, enter and continue along the path to the next waymark at the end of the wood. Turn right as directed before descending then ascending to the edge of the woods (Bettws Dingle) and a further fingerpost, with derelict farm buildings on the right.

Continue straight on to the next stile, maintaining the same direction with a fence on the left. At the next fingerpost turn left down a track to a further fingerpost to a stile and lane. Turn right descending to the main road (A438 ④). Turn right and walk for approximately 300m to a fingerpost on the right-hand road verge directing you left into a field. Entering the field, descend the steep slope with the river visible to the left. Continue past the fingerpost ahead, still descending, parallel to the river. Over the stile and footbridge in the far left-hand corner of a field turn right, with a stream on the right. Walk slightly away from the stream to locate a stile in a fence. Crossing the stile, head towards some farm buildings. Pass through the farm complex and on to a further stile into a field, regaining your previous direction.

Cross the field to a waymark in the hedge and continue across fields and stiles to a green lane and turn left. At a T-junction in the green lane follow the waymark into a field (straight on) where the path follows the line of a hedge on the right. Pass over the next stile and cross the next field, bearing slightly left towards the river. Follow the riverbank path (elevated in places) through a wooded area to join the B4351. Turn left over the bridge and head into Hay-on-Wye.

Section 12
Hay-on-Wye to Glasbury

Distance:	8km (5 miles)
Grade:	Easy
Terrain:	Footpaths, riverside, verges to busy road, field paths
OS Map:	OS Explorers 201: Knighton and Presteigne or 188: Builth Wells
Route Map:	Map 8; Page 45
Guide Time:	2 hours

Cross the river bridge ❶ on the B4351 and head up the road (NW) along the ascending footpath for 270m to a stile on the left. Cross and follow the hedge/fence line along the field edge (WSW) to a further stile by a wall on the right, with the River Wye in front. Continue, following waymarks along the wall edge, descending to a stile and footbridge. Cross the stile and turn left, following a track past a cottage to the riverside. Continue for approximately 2.25km and then diagonally cross a field to steps and a stile. Turn left alongside the A438

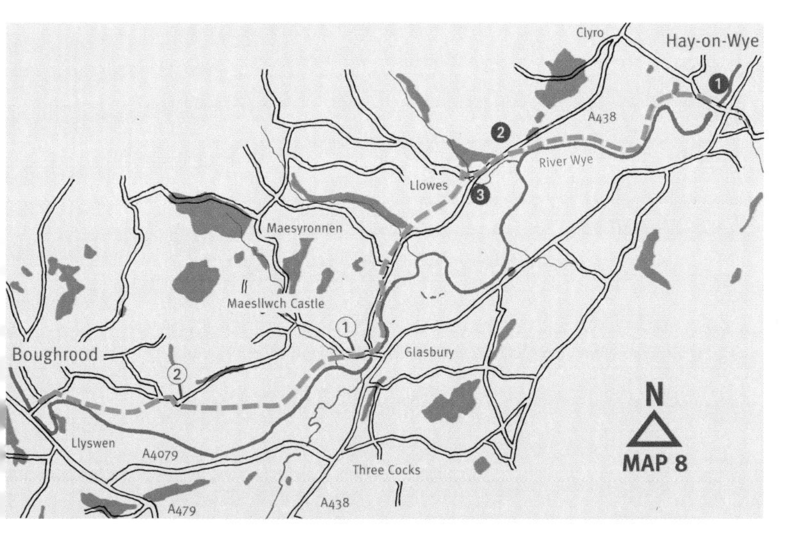

❷, emerging onto the road and crossing to the other side.

Turn left and continue into the village of Llowes. At a telephone box opposite the Radnor Arms ❸ go right, following the waymark, and ascend the road to reach a stile on the left by a metal gate. Cross a further stile and ascend the field beyond the fence line to cross a stile at Bryn yr Hydd Common. Follow the waymarks through a farmyard onto a descending lane to the main road. Cross and turn right along the verge for approximately 750m to a waymarked kissing gate on the left. Go through this and on to two further kissing gates into a field. Turn right (SSE) to the river's edge and a path leading onto the main road at Glasbury Bridge. At the bridge cross the road and go through the car park opposite, continuing past the toilets and joining a road into the village.

Section 13
Glasbury to Boughrood Bridge

Distance:	5.2km (3¼ miles)
Grade:	Easy
Terrain:	Byway, track, footpaths, field and riverside walking. Short sections of quiet road following the Wye Valley Walk
OS Map:	OS Explorer 188: Builth Wells
Route Map:	Map 8; Page 45
Guide Time:	1½ hours

From the Maesllwch Arms ①, head W along the road to the first bend and to a fingerpost. Turn left along the track to a river path and onto a stone track. Keep on the track, past a house and through metal gates, onto a grassy track with a hedge on the right and go over a stile and along the field edge, through a gate and into a lane. Head W at a sharp bend in the lane and take the right turn at a waymark through a gate still heading W. Continue along a further green lane and field to join a hedge on the right leading onto a road (B4350) at Pistyll Farm ②. Turn left along the metalled road to Boughrood Brest. At the first houses on the left, turn left by a fingerpost and pass between cottages, through a gate onto a green lane and further open field. Keep to the hedge on the right towards a stile into the next field. With the river on the left, go through a gate and along a green lane with the river below. At the waymark descend to the riverside path and emerge onto a road, turning left into Boughrood village over the river bridge. If the footpath here is flooded, follow another footpath along through a gate and Old Rectory Gardens onto the road to turn left into Boughrood.

Rapids on the River Wye

Section 14
Boughrood Bridge to Builth Wells

Distance:	19.3km (12 miles)
Grade:	Easy/moderate
Terrain:	Riverside tracks and footpaths, quiet lanes, hillsides and rough grassland, following the Wye Valley Walk
Maps:	OS Explorer 188: Builth Wells
Route Map:	Map 9: Page 49
Guide Time:	5½ hours

Leaving Boughrood Bridge ❶, cross over the river and turn right at a fingerpost. Follow along the river edge, through a gate onto the riverside path and continue for 2km.

At Sgithwen Brook ❷ turn left and follow the brook to the main road (A470). Turn right, along the road, and cross the Llanstephan suspension bridge – one of last wooden-decked suspension bridges in Wales. Continue along the road over an old railway bridge and go left at a T-junction, following the road and passing between old bridge abutments. Turn left over a stile immediately after a waymarker post. Follow the track along the riverside until it opens into a small field. Bear right to a gate and footbridge over the river, cross and ascend by an old railway viaduct to a stile on the left. Cross and turn right along the road for approximately 1.5km towards the old railway station. Just before the station take the left-hand waymarked, descending path to the road. Turn right over Erwood Bridge ❸ and proceed across the road to join a minor road and ascend to Twmpath Common over a cattle grid. At the 'Twmpath' sign turn right at a fingerpost and head NW to follow a waymarker post and descend to a stile. Cross the stile and follow the tree-lined path and a further waymarker descending and rising to a fingerpost and then descending to a gate and stile with a stream on the right.

Cross the stream via a footbridge and turn right to ascend to a road. Turn left at a waymark, rising past a house on the left and continuing steeply to Little Hill Common. At the top stay on an undulating metalled road for approximately 1.5km. At a fingerpost on the left take the rising stone track on the left marked 'Old Bedw'. Keep straight ahead,

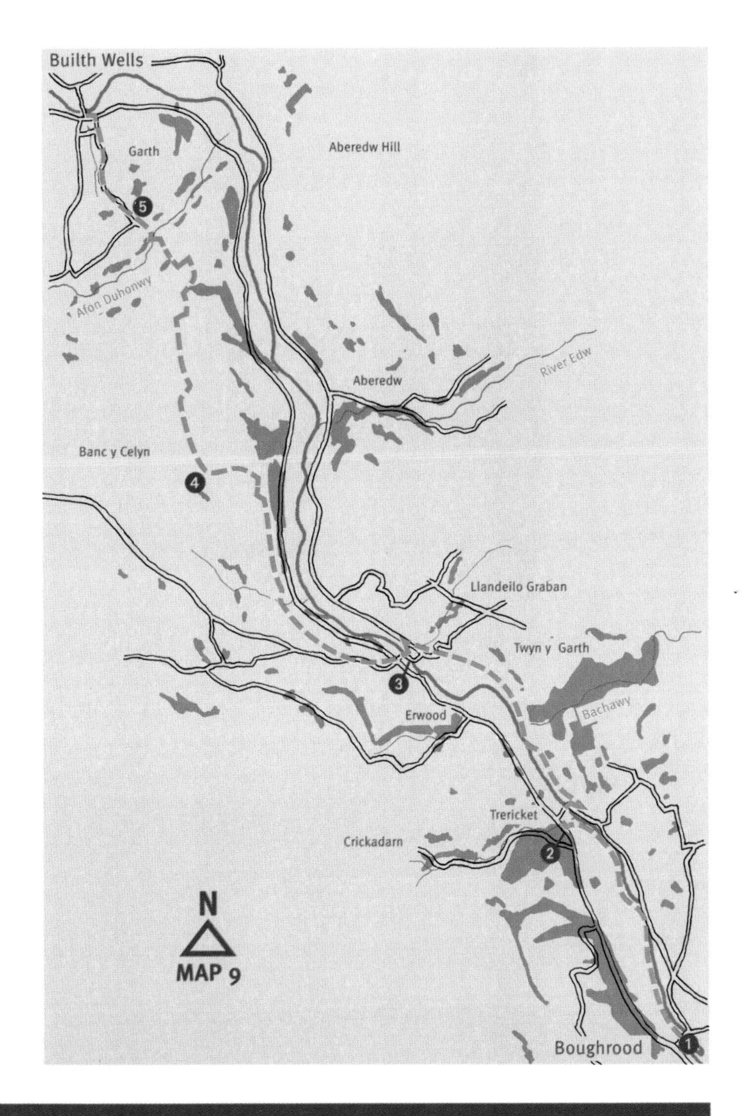

leaving the stone track on the right and onto a grass track to reach a gate with a rising track ahead. Keep to the left-hand track following a fence on the left. At the top of the rise, by a fingerpost ❹, bear right heading N past a further finger-post and head NNW over undulating ground crossing two streams and arriving at a small pool with a fingerpost in front and a gate beyond.

Through the gate bear right alongside an old hedge on the right to reach a small pool to the right. Continue up to two metal gates and beyond, through a common and onto an undulating grassy track to a gate. Go through the gate and keep to the fence line on the right, descending. Keeping to the right at a fingerpost, descend to a wooden gate and continue beyond on a grassy stone track through two gates to another stone track.

Descend to a minor road and cross into a grassy lane. At the next junction turn left and continue to a minor road. Turn right just before reaching the road and go down a sunken lane at a waymarked fingerpost, past a white cottage on the left. Go through a wooden gate and over a footbridge to an ascend-ing metalled road, which bears round to the left.

At a T-junction ❺ turn right past Newry Farm and over Gloew Brook and Tanhouse Bridge into the outskirts of Builth Wells. At the T-junction turn right along Castle Road into the town centre.

The bridge over the Wye in Builth Wells

Section 15
Builth Wells to Newbridge-on-Wye

Distance:	11.7km (7¼ miles)
Grade:	Easy
Terrain:	Mainly riverside footpaths and tracks, two short sections of road walking, following the Wye Valley Walk
Maps:	OS Explorer 200: Llandrindod Wells and Elan Valley
Route Map:	Map 10; Page 51
Guide Time:	3 hours

Starting from the main car park and information centre ❶ close to the public toilets, locate the path alongside the west bank of the river and proceed NW past the rugby pitches. Continue on this clearly marked path parallel to the river for some distance, following it to the left to negotiate a bridge over a tributary of the main river, through a kissing gate into a field and back towards the river. Over the next stile and footbridge, maintain the same bearing, keeping close to the river. Cross a further stile into a wooded area following the track close to the river and, keeping to this track, go under a railway bridge ❷, maintaining the same direction.

Continue to a cattle grid and go straight over, keeping the riverside track heading. Cross a number of stiles then a further stile and footbridge into a wood. The track gradually

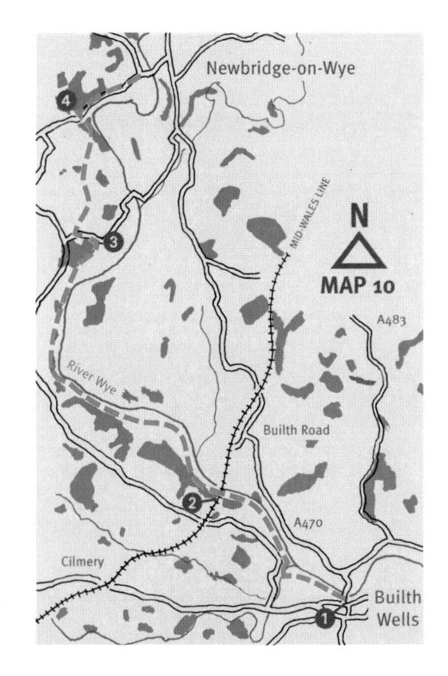

heads away from the river but continues along the edge of a wooded area. Be careful to locate a shingle bungalow down on your right close to the river. Head towards this, following the path to locate a stile, then go past the bungalow near to a stream. After crossing a footbridge walk along the edge of the wood with the stream on your left and a farm ahead (Bryn-wern Hall) heading NNE. Over the next stile, keep the post-and-wire fence close to your right-hand side, heading towards a farm. Go through the waymarked gates following the signs into a farmyard then immediately head left up to a stile on the edge of the wood. Follow the path through the wood to a stile on the other side and onto a metalled road ❸.

Turn left along the road past a sign to Trederwen on your left, and past a post box and cottage also on the left. Look out for a waymark on the right and follow this off the road on a path along the edge of a wood heading N. Locate a stile in a hedge in the corner of a field and cross this to follow a hedge on the right heading NNE. Go through the next waymarked gateway, keeping the hedge on your left, again on a NNE bearing and locating a stile ahead by a large oak tree. After crossing the stile, continue on the same heading across an open field towards trees, to locate a further stile. Continue, crossing a path, a small stream and another stile, and bear N, down to a footbridge over a small river.

Continue up a steep bank keeping the hedge to your left and locate a further gate. Pass through and, on the same bearing, maintain the hedge to your left. Go through the next metal gate and then locate a stile adjoining a further gate (note the large house on the opposite bank straight ahead). Maintain the same N bearing into woods below, over a waymarked stile, following the clear track through a wood (much of the track is on pontoons over a very wet area). Fork left at a waymarker post and go up the rise to reach the road over a stile to turn right along the B4358 ❹.

Continue along the road towards Newbridge-on-Wye. Cross the bridge into the village.

Section 16
Newbridge-on-Wye to Rhayader

Distance:	15.3km (9½ miles)
Grade:	Easy/moderate
Terrain:	Quiet lanes, footpaths, byway, riverside, fields and low hill walking, following the Wye Valley Walk
OS Maps:	OS Explorer 200: Llandrindod Wells and Elan Valley
Route Map:	Map 11: Page 54
Guide Time:	4 hours

Leave the village ❶ via the river bridge on the B4358, heading WSW. After 100m take the right turn into a quiet lane.

Continue along the road for approximately 800m and look out for a post box in the right-hand bank and, shortly after, a waymarked stile to your right. Enter the woods heading N. Cross a double footbridge and go up a bank, locating a stile in the hedge ahead. Over this, follow the hedge on your right on the edge of woodland. Continue over further stiles towards the properties ahead. At a left-hand property (Ty'n-y-coed ❷) turn left along the track for a short distance, turning right over a stile alongside a gate, heading NW.

Continue on this heading over a number of stiles to a waymarker post in a line of trees (in a gully) by a large stream. Cross the bridge, turning right to a stile up a steep bank. Over the stile, head across the field NNW and towards a stile in the top right-hand corner. Cross the stile onto a metalled road at a T-junction with a farm drive (Upper Cefncoed) and head straight on (N).

Continue down the road noting the stream on your left as the road turns E towards the River Wye. Before reaching the river cross the bridge on your left over the stream and, after a very short distance, continue straight on ignoring the tarmac track going left (to Tycwtta). Continue on this track to double gates, taking the wooden one on the left to continue up the slope. Follow the rising path through the next wooden gate and maintain your bearing on this track with the River Wye parallel on the right-hand side.

Follow the main track, ignoring those to the left and keep the post-and-wire fence immediately to your right as you skirt the lower contours of Trembyd. When the path descends, again ignore the tracks to the left but keep to the main path with a stone wall immediately on the right. On reaching a wooden gate on the descending path, pass through onto a metalled road ❸ and continue on the same bearing. The road turns left, passing Hodrid House on the right, and then descends steeply towards the river. Keep on this road passing a large property on the left and The Mill, to reach the village of Llanwrthwl ❹.

Proceed to a T-junction and turn left past houses and a

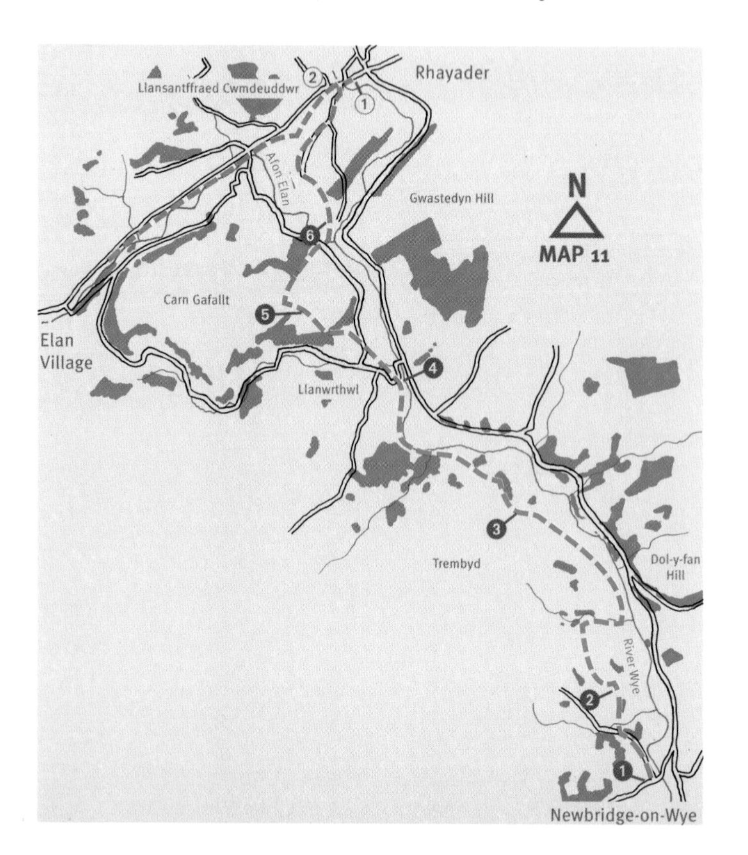

Approaching Rhayader

school on the right. Follow the sign for Elan Village and, after a short distance, take the track to the right at a left-hand bend, away from the metalled road. Continue up the rising track until reaching another road turning left. After some 50m turn right following the waymarked rising track which continues up for some distance to Cefn ❺.

At the high point of this section continue on the clear track WNW through a farmyard. Watch for, and take, a waymarked right turn 300m after Cefn, NNE past the approach to Pen-y-rhiw. As you begin to descend towards a wood, ignore the stile and wooden gate to the left, and proceed straight on (NE) along the edge of the wood. Continue down the track, keeping the woodland on the left, to a gate and into a narrow track down to a further gate leading to a metalled road.

Turn right by Wernnewydd and head towards the River Wye. At the river bank turn left (NW) and follow the waymark sign, keeping close to the post and pig netting fence on the left and following the track towards a footbridge (Glyn Bridge) over the River Elan. This is a large suspended footbridge given to some movement. Turn right over the bridge and locate a track heading NNE, up towards a farm. Through the gate, enter the farmyard, turning right and continuing along the metalled road close to the river.

Follow this road until reaching a wood on the left ❻. Turn left down the waymarked grassy track and, on reaching a dismantled railway line, bear right, parallel to the line, along a track heading NW. Pass through a gate and bear right to a stone track and left through a farmyard. After another gate take the track heading NNE.

Continue on the track until you reach a metalled road and head straight on this road towards Rhayader into the town, passing New House.

Section 17
Rhayader to Elan Valley

Distance:	4.8km (3 miles)
Grade:	Very easy
Terrain:	Made up pathways
Maps:	OS Explorer 200: Llandrindod Wells and Elan Valley
Route Map:	Map 11; Page 54
Guide Time:	1 hour

Leave Rhayader ① on the B4518 (signposted to Elan Valley), passing the Triangle Inn on the left on the outskirts of the town. Proceed along the left-hand side of the B4518 passing 'Llawrllan' and continue for a further 50m before locating a clearly signed trail on the left ②. Follow this trail passing the rear of a row of houses and continuing on a 2m wide tarmac surface in a SSW direction. The trail continues for about 4km, running parallel to the B4518 at a varying distance and, at times, right alongside it. In the main however, it runs close but with a hedge and trees between you and the road. You are following the line of a disused railway, passing through an area owned by the local Wildlife Trust. Many of the trees contain nest boxes. After some 4km you will locate the Elan Valley Hotel.

Elan Village can be reached by continuing for a further 750m.

Above the Elan Valley

Elan Valley

This is a really lovely picturesque location. A 'Welsh Lake District' giving spectacular contrasts between natural moors and woodlands and man-made lakes.

Just before the beginning of the last century, when the city of Birmingham's increasing heavy industry and rising population needed far more water than could be provided by its own natural wells, the city's corporation decided to construct three major dams and drown the Elan Valley. Work started in 1893, when a constructor's railway was built to facilitate the movement of labour and materials to the sites. At any one time, about 5,000 men were employed on the project, which eventually created the four reservoirs of Caban-Coch, Garreg-ddu, Pen-y-Garreg and finally the highest, Craig Coch. The route of this railway, which was of standard gauge and connected to the main line, is today used as a walk, bike or bridle pathway. There are several easy-access parking and picnic sites at the dams or close by. The dams and reservoirs were officially opened by King Edward VII and Queen Alexandra in 1904. A further scheme, the more westerly Claerwen Reservoir and dam, was completed in 1952 and opened by Queen Elizabeth II shortly after she became the new monarch. The first class Elan Valley Visitor Centre, just 5km (3 miles) out of the local town of Rhayader on the B4518, remains open seven days a week between mid March and late October. It's a must for everything you need to know about the 113 sq km (70 sq miles) estate.

Rhayader, at the foot of the valley, is a friendly, atmospheric town. It's a real gem, dating from the 5th century AD, with a lot of decidedly lawless history. The town was once a staging post on the old coaching route between London and Aberystwyth and a number of historic coaching inns remain. Accommodation is generally plentiful with caravan parks, holiday cottages, hotels and inexpensive B&Bs. There's a variety of eating places too, from cafés and small restaurants to pubs and no shortage of gift shops either! Within a short distance of the centre, there is the Welsh Royal Crystal Factory with its showroom, the Wye-side River Walk with a little pebble beach and picnic area, and the Red Kite Centre at Gigrin Farm. Also not too far is the castle mound overlooking the River Wye, built in 1178 but destroyed during the siege of 1231.

Section 18
Elan to Pont-rhyd-y-groes

Distance:	29km (18 miles)
Grade:	Moderate/tough
Terrain:	Metalled road, bridleway, byway, track, footpaths, marshy ground and rough grassland
Maps:	OS Explorers 200: Llandrindod Wells and Elan Valley and 213: Aberystwyth and Cwm Rheidol
Route Map:	Map 12; Page 60
Guide Time:	9 hours

Leave Elan Village ❶ and follow the B4518 in a SW direction. Continue past the dam on the left ❷ and a disused quarry on the right, following a tarmac path alongside the reservoir edge. Take the bridge across the reservoir signposted to Garreg-ddu and, approximately 60m past a chapel, pass through a gate on the right and follow an ascending woodland bridleway in a roughly SW direction.

Soon after crossing over a vehicle track the bridleway turns W to reach the edge of the woodland at a gate. Through the gate, continue W along the edge of the wood passing masts at the top of a rise. On reaching a gravel road cross the stream and go through a metal gate. Descend to a waymark turning right and keeping the pine coppice on your left, follow waymarks down towards a road ❸.

Head W along the road for approximately 100m to reach a fork. Take the right fork to Claerwen Dam. Do not cross the dam but continue on the byway along the edge of the reservoir. After approximately 10km the byway reaches a gated bridge at GR SN819672, just beyond the track to Claerwen Farm ❹.

Cross the bridge and follow a shale road in a roughly WNW direction, ignoring the bridle-way veering off to the SW. After a while the track reaches a point where a tarmac surface has been laid. This eventually becomes a metalled road leading W. Approximately 700m after crossing the second cattle grid, at GR SN756682 ❺, turn right (heading NNE) on a metalled road.

At the end of the coniferous plantation, pass through a gate and head NNE on a bridleway for 1.3km to reach Blaen-Marchnant. From here the rutted bridleway changes direction to WNW. This twisting track is followed until a metal gate is reached at GR SN756711 ❻. Pass through the gate and turn immediately right (N) keeping the fence on your

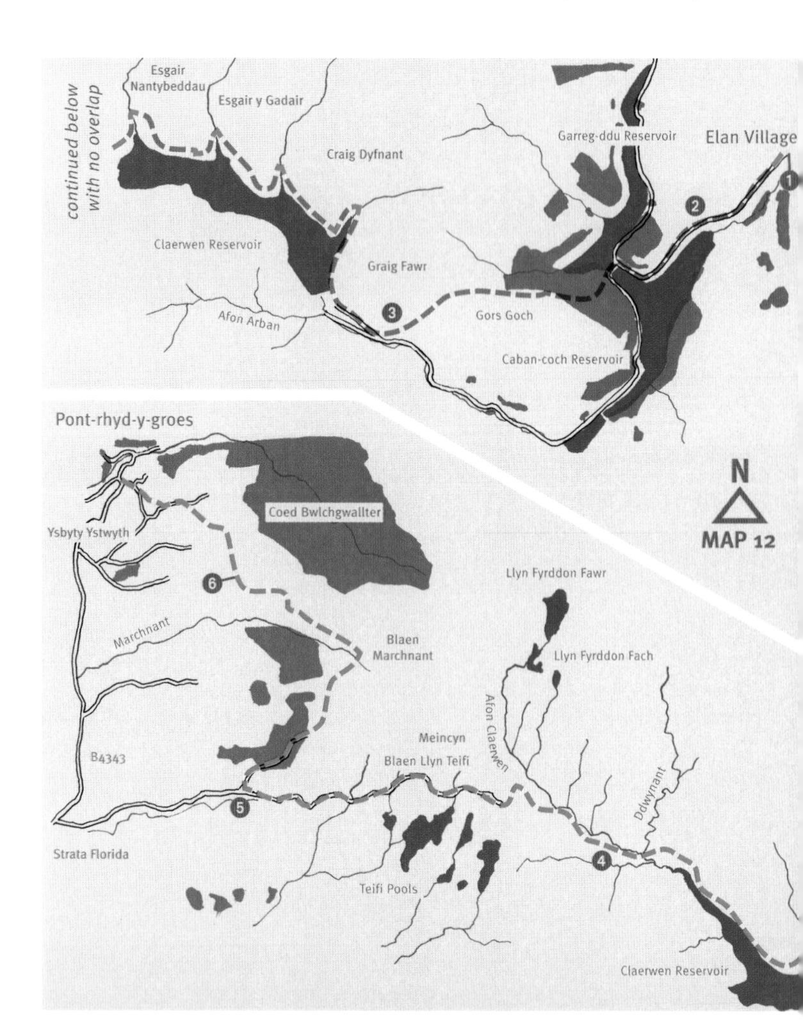

right. Pass beyond a junction of fences and, keeping a small hill (spot height 357m) to the left, follow the track around, first W then changing to NW, passing the small hillside holding of Hafod-y-gau-uchaf. Continue on this track which descends to join a metalled road. Turn left (WSW) for 300m then cross a stile on the right and bear WNW to reach a small lane beyond a stream and tiny wooded area. Turn right along the lane and proceed into the village of Pont-rhyd-y-groes.

Section 19
Pont-rhyd-y-groes to Devil's Bridge

Distance:	13.7km (8½ miles)
Grade:	Moderate
Terrain:	Riverside and forestry tracks and paths, metalled roads, footpaths and rough grassland
Maps:	OS Explorer 213: Aberystwyth and Cwm Rheidol
Route Map:	Map 13; Page 62
Guide Time:	4½ hours

Head NW out of the village. Take the waymarked, ascending path on the right just before the river bridge at GR SN742728 ❶ on the south side of the river (do not cross the bridge). Cross the stile with the river and valley on the left and a white cottage on the crest. Do not cross the fence/stile on the right.

Continue towards a cottage and past a derelict building to a stile and yellow waymark in front of a cottage. Crossing the stile, pass through the cottage garden (left) to a footbridge, stile and a wooden gate. Continue straight on, descending through a wooded area, over wooden boards and crossing a stile into a wood with the river on the left. The path continues (indistinctly in places) through pine woodland with rising ground on the right. Cross a rustic footbridge ❷ over a stream passing a river footbridge (left) and following a maroon waymark over a further rustic bridge. The path emerges onto a forestry road at a waymark. Continue E ignoring the rising waymarked path on the right. Eventually a forestry road merges from the right. Continue on a track, turning right before a metal bridge and over a stile into an ascending field.

Head NNE through the field with a fence on the left and a waymark midway with a stile beyond. Cross the stile and descend, with a river bridge (Pont Dologau) on the left. Turn right onto a stone track with a white cottage on the right, go through a wooden gate and follow the beech wood edge. Continue to a fork in the track opposite a bow in the river. Take the descending track on the left beside Dol-chenog ❸. Pass through the yard and turn right along the stone track leading to a bridge. Cross and proceed up a metalled road to a T-junction turning left through Cwmystwyth to a former chapel on the left and Y-Fron to the right (GR SN785742 ❹).

Take the ascending stone track at Y-Fron and pass a white cottage on the right to a waymarked wooden gate. Follow the falling edge of the stream on the right to a cottage (Ty'n-y-rhyd). Cross the footbridge and go up the steps to a path in front of a gate. Pass through a wooden gate to the left, crossing the stream and through a wicket gate at the back of the cottage, heading NW to a marker post. Cross the marshy ground going NW to reach a stile, then a further stile on the same heading, rising to a stile on the right. Continue up

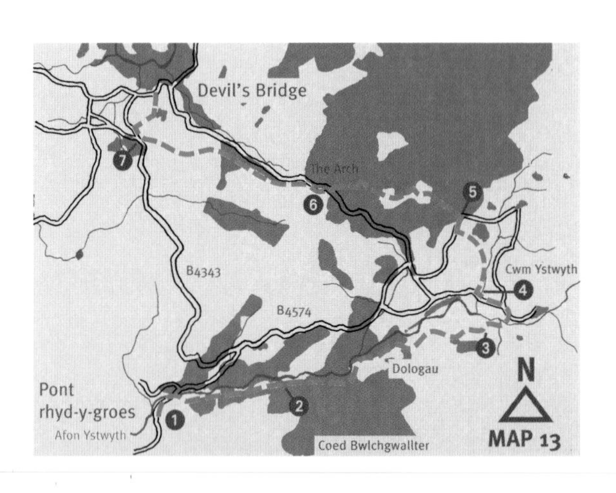

to a further stile crossing onto a metalled road.

Turn right past a marker post on the left and, at a bend in the road, take the waymarked forestry path 5 descending W. Cross the main track and follow another waymarked path (WNW) over a footbridge onto a waymarked stone road. Turn left then, after 50m, right at Gelmast Farm. Pass through the farmyard following a waymarker onto a rising track. Continue through a wooden gate into a conifer plantation on a NW heading.

At a junction (GR SN765757) turn left towards a picnic area and The Arch 6. Turn right through The Arch along the road and take the bridle track through a gate left of the road, running parallel with the road. At a fork keep right and continue through a forested area and continue WNW until the track joins the B4343 road 7. Turn right along the road and, at the first sharp bend, just past a school, between a house and a bungalow, go through the gate onto a grassy tree lined track. After approximately 200m look for a waymark post between trees on the left. Head N to a further waymark on the left between trees. Continue N to a waymark with a wire fence on the right then another waymark and stile.

Cross the stile onto a stone road and emerge onto the A4120 at Devil's Bridge.

Section 20
Devil's Bridge to Ponterwyd

Distance:	8km (5 miles)
Grade:	Moderate
Terrain:	Steep footpaths through woodlands, quiet lanes and tracks
Maps:	OS Explorer 213: Aberystwyth and Cwm Rheidol
Route Map:	Map 14; Page 64
Guide Time:	3 hours

Leave Devil's Bridge ❶ along the A4120 heading W. Upon reaching the end of the 30mph speed restriction, take the waymarked path through a wooden gate on the right and follow the waymark N then NW to a wooded area. At a fork take the left path, ascending over a bluff to a path, which follows a railway fence to the next waymark. Continue upwards to the next post and a further post, and then descend to a waterfall and footbridge. Cross the footbridge and take the path to the right, following the railway line on the right. Cross the railway line at a waymarked crossing ❷ (beware of trains) and descend through a wooded area to the valley bottom, following the waymarks to a footbridge over the river ❸. Turn right along the metalled road and rise up to a road marked 'Unsuitable for Motor Vehicles'. Continue

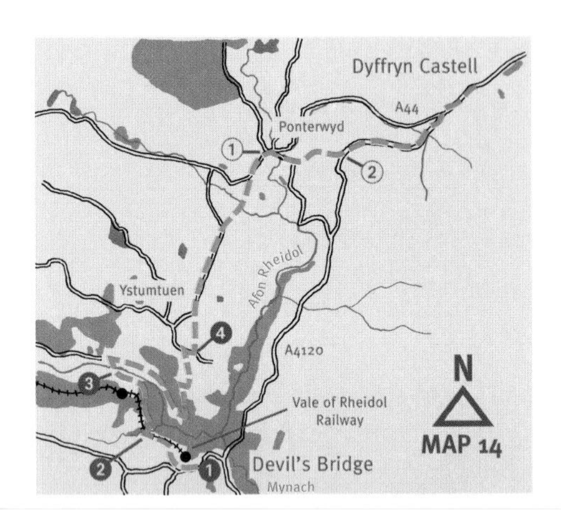

along this road to arrive at a junction with a field on the right. Follow the path with a field fence on the right. Directly opposite a house in a field, take the rising path through the trees to a track which turns N to rise steeply to a stile and wire fence. Go due E still rising steeply up the saddle of a field and continue, as the path levels, to reach a waymarked standing stone, marking a crossing track. Turn left along this waymarked track to a farm with a waymarked gate on the right.

Go through the gate heading E across a field to a footbridge, before ascending to a stile and road beyond ❹. Turn left along the road and head N. Just before a second cattle grid take the descending waymarked path on the right through two wicket gates to emerge onto the A44 at Ponterwyd. Turn right and walk into the village.

Section 21
Ponterwyd to Dyffryn Castell

Distance:	3.2km (2 miles)
Grade:	Easy
Terrain:	Metalled road and bridleway
Maps:	OS Explorer 213: Aberystwyth and Cwm Rheidol
Route Map:	Map 14; Page 64
Guide Time:	1 hour

Leave the village ① heading NE along the busy A44 and go right at the first road junction, passing the post office on the left. Turn left onto a bridleway just before the first right-hand bend in the road. After passing the works yard on the right, go through a gate following the path ENE. Pass through two further gates and then a wicket gate with a rising path across a field. Continue in the same direction to reach a waymarked bridle path and gate at the fence line. Emerge onto a metalled road (B4343 ②) turn left and join the A44 after approximately 1km. Turn right along the A44 to Dyffryn Castell. Take great care here as the verge is very narrow.

The Dyffryn Castell Hotel

Plynlimon

Plynlimon is not so much a mountain as a high moorland plateau, best known as the source of the River Severn which flows for 354km (220 miles) and is the longest river in Britain. It is also the source of the River Wye which, after following a very different route of 210km (130 miles), south-easterly, eventually flows into the Severn Estuary at Chepstow, just as it widens into the Bristol Channel. The fast flowing River Rheidol also begins on these wild moors. It tumbles through the dramatic gorge and waterfalls at Devil's Bridge, before discharging into the sea at Aberystwyth. Over its short course of only 40km (25 miles) it falls some 518m (1,700ft).

The highest point of Plynlimon (or Pumlumon Fawr) is at 752m (2,468ft), but the source of the Severn is in a peaty, boggy area at 610m (2,000ft), where guide posts indicate a small pool out of which the embryonic brook of the Severn can be seen leaving to start its long journey. Not far away to the east of Plynlimon the river Clywedog flows into the Llyn Clywedog Reservoir. Its dam regulates the flow of the Clywedog and therefore also the Severn, of which it is a tributary. This reservoir, just above Llanidloes, can also be reached by car via a pretty drive from Machynlleth.

Hafren, the Welsh name for the River Severn, possibly has its origin in Roman times. Severn may be derived from Sabrina, which in turn is derived from Habren (Hafren), who was the daughter of Locrinus, the eldest son of Brutus who gave his name to Britain after leading the Trojans to what was then called Albion. Elsewhere, in Arthurian fable, Plynlimon is described as the 'highest wind in the world', a recognition of its exposed location.

Until the 19th century there were silver and lead mines on the slopes of the Rheidol Valley and there is a museum of that era at Llanwernog. There's also an interesting visitor centre at Nant-yr-Arian.

Section 22
Dyffryn Castell to Machynlleth

Distance:	32.2km (20 miles)
Grade:	Tough
Terrain:	Exposed, remote high-level footpaths, steep rough grassland and marshy, boggy terrain, areas with no defined paths; bridleways, tracks and quiet lanes. Note: Due to the distance, remoteness and exposure, together with the sections of indistinct or non-existent tracks, skill with map and compass is needed, particularly in bad weather
Maps:	OS Explorers 213: Aberystwyth and Cwm Rheidol and 215: Newtown and Machynlleth
Route Map:	Map 15; Page 67–8
Guide Time:	10 hours

This section of the walk involves a long steady day and starts at Dyffryn Castell Hotel ❶. Head NE along the A44 for approximately 60m to cross a stile on the left, just beyond some buildings. On entering a field continue up with Nant Bowen down in a gully on the left.

Bear NNE to negotiate two further stiles before crossing a grassy marsh area to a fourth stile into a field, with a wire fence to the right. Shortly, leave the fence and traverse steeply up left (N) to one remaining stile and climb up through grass and heather to the ridge.

The path continues along the ridge, just below the crest and parallel with the A44, crossing two wet gullies before skirting right around a bluff. In poor weather exercise care here as the ridge drops away steeply.

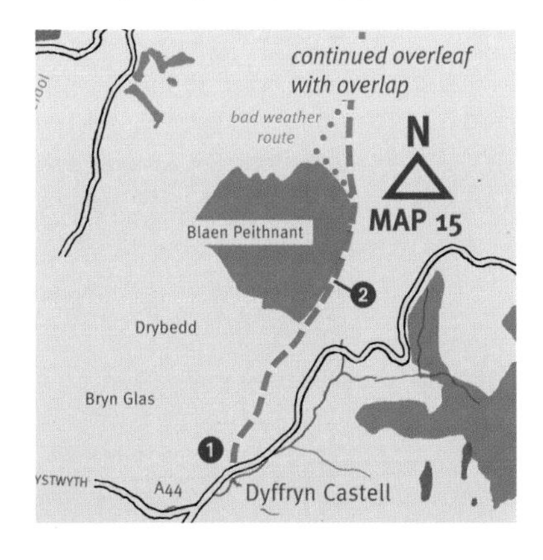

Climb steadily over undulating, sometimes boggy, rough grassy terrain to reach a perimeter wire fence along the Forestry Commission fir plantation of Blaen-Peithnant on the left ❷.

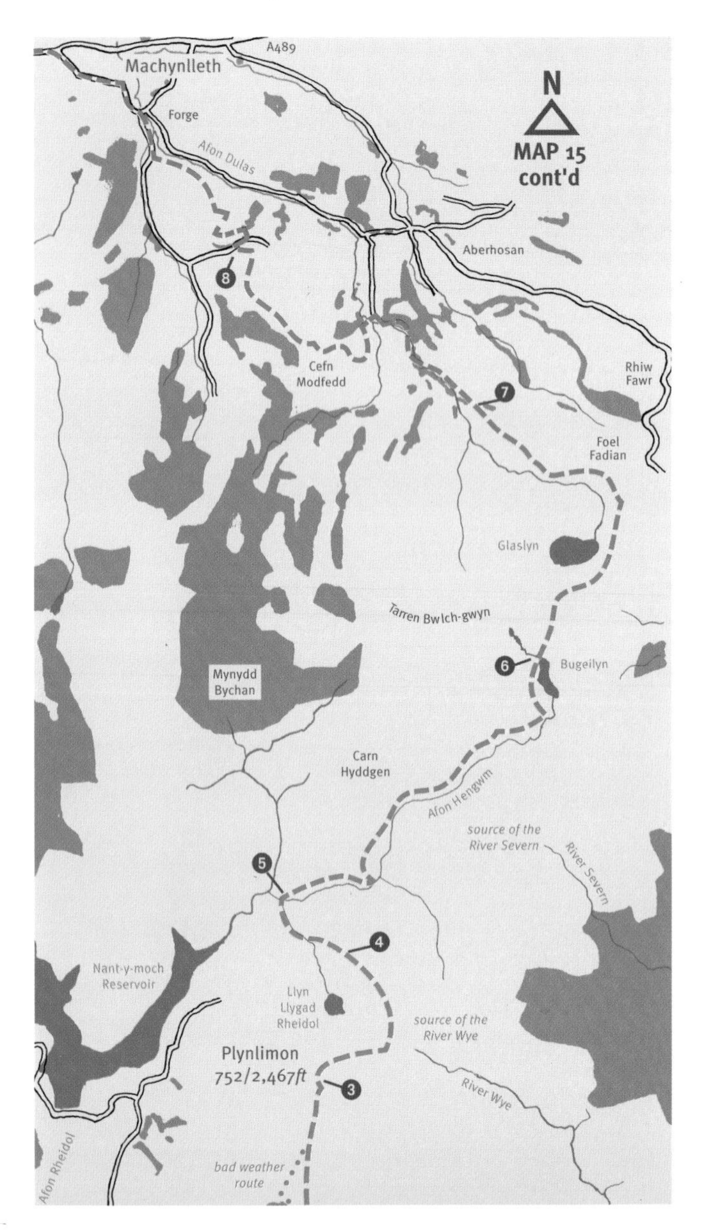

Cross the fence and continue to follow as it progresses further left, N and NNW. The footpath then crosses a T-junction in the fence via a gate at GR SN787846.

In fine weather take the path veering right (N) on the mostly well-defined track up the ridge, following cairn markers for a little over 2km to the summit of Plynlimon ❸. In bad weather, you can err on the side of safety by following the fence to the left up to a ridge where the plantation ends, then go right, following a further fence NNE for almost 2km to the summit. Whichever route you choose, just beyond the summit, cross the wire fence via a stile to the left to find a trig point and several stone windbreak shelters.

Follow the wire fence NE to arrive shortly at a further cairn and follow the fence as it veers right, E and ENE, to descend gradually for approximately 800m to reach a cairn.

From this point, where the fence veers SE, go directly N (no path here) and descend gently over rough, grassy ground for about 750m to join a wire fence coming from the right. Keeping this fence on your right, continue NW.

At GR SN793885 ❹ the fence starts to veer more towards NNW. Here leave the fence and bear more WNW, picking your way down to the left of the rock outcrops to reach a footpath.

Head NNW to a small stand of fir trees enclosed by a low stone wall, just before the footbridge at GR SN785892 ❺. Cross the footbridge over the River Hengwm and climb the fence on the opposite bank to join a footpath under a rocky outcrop heading NE. This footpath is not marked on the map. Turning ENE the path runs parallel with the river (down on the right). Continue for about 1km under Banc Lluestnewydd to arrive at a derelict stone cottage and pens on the right at GR SN796895. You will see waterfalls on the opposite side of the river to the SE. Head NNE and NE up the valley, walking over mixed ground and gullies. At GR SN815916 go right (E) to join a stone track which skirts around the base of a hill, passing Bugeilyn lake on the right, to reach a bridge and boat house ❻.

Continue along the track passing a derelict stone cottage and a new barn on the left. The route progresses past the eastern side of the expansive lake Glaslyn.

Approximately 500m after the lake car park entrance, look out for a marker post on the left at GR SN832947. Here, leave the main track and head off NNW on the well-signed Glyndwr's Way. Follow the rutted track as it gently rises up, then left in a westerly direction, below Foel Fadian. To the left is a deep gully carrying the infant Afon Dulas. The clear route goes over a rise to reveal impressive views in good weather.

At a marker post at GR SN826952 take the left fork on a descending zig-zag track. At the bottom of the rocky descent, the path heads NW down a beautiful valley on a mainly grassy section with fields, mixed trees and, if the day is clear, views of Cadair Idris and Snowdonia in the distance. Continue along this scenic route for 1.5km passing

Machynlleth

Machynlleth is a small market town with a population of about 2,200. There is a long history of human activity in the area and even legends linking it with a fertile plain now lost under the waters of Cardigan Bay. Bronze Age people mined copper here and the Romans built a fort near by. Edward I granted a charter in 1291 to hold a market every Wednesday and this is still held today. Owain Glyndŵr was crowned Prince of Wales in 1404 near Parliament House which is one of three medieval houses still to be seen. Royal House is believed to be where Charles I stayed in 1643.

Featuring most prominently, at the end of a wide main street, is a magnificent 24m (80ft) clock tower which forms the hub of the town. The tower was built in 1874 to mark the coming of age of Lord Castlereagh, eldest son of the Marquess of Londonderry, who lived at Y Plas. This fine residence at present houses Celtica, an impressive Welsh heritage centre. The varied local architecture is enhanced by one of the most spacious and attractive main streets in Wales. In this street can also be found the tourist information centre, with excellent parking facilities near by. The town is a most inviting and pleasant place to visit and explore and visitors will enjoy its wide range of shops, bars and restaurants.

Machynlleth offers a wide range of activities to visitors. It is close to the coast, local nature reserves and a seemingly endless choice of riverside and hill walks. There are plenty of places to enjoy meals and the town offers a high standard of accommodation. The town is well served by the Cambrian Coast railway and there is no shortage of buses and taxis. Near by is the Centre for Advanced Technology which promotes more sustainable life styles, both new and traditional.

through several gates to reach Esgair-Fochnant ❼.

Pass the farm and follow the track a further 200m to Nantyfyda. In front of the house the track hairpins right and becomes a metalled lane. Follow this lane, which winds uphill and, at the first road junction, ignore the right fork and continue ahead NW for almost 2km to reach a telephone box at a junction.

Continue past the telephone box on your left then, after 50m, take the left turn at a T-junction, crossing a bridge over the river.

Continue on this steep lane to a farm at the crest. Turn right and follow the waymarks through the farmyard of Cleiriau-isaf. Leave the farm and follow a clear route up to a metal-gated track, which initially heads NW, but soon turns W.

At a point where the track turns sharply SSW look out for a marker post. Here, leave the main track and head up a grass bank (NW) to reach two gates at a field corner. Go through the gate on the right and bear NW, diagonally across a field, through a further gate before following a clear rutted grass bridleway.

At GR SN779977 the bridleway joins a track and heads off in a northerly direction. The track follows roughly the hill contours round to the W to emerge at a narrow lane at Blaen-pant ❽. Turn right along the lane ENE until the first road junction. Here turn left, to follow the snaking road over two cattle grids before the well surfaced lane turns N to arrive at Henllan Farm.

Follow the waymarks W through the farmyard, before heading initially in a northerly direction on a wide, clear but often muddy track. The track traverses down into the valley and follows parallel to the river for approximately 1km to reach a road.

At the road turn right (NNW) and follow it for about 2.25km, passing the golf course to arrive at the eastern end of Machynlleth at a T-junction. Turn left along the A489 into the centre of the town where food and accommodation are available.

Section 23
Machynlleth to Abergynolwyn

Distance:	11.7km (7¼ miles)
Grade:	Moderate
Terrain:	Mainly hillside forestry tracks and footpaths, short road section to begin followed by steep quiet lane
Maps:	OS Explorer OL23: Cadair Idris and Bala Lake
Route Map:	Map 16; Page 73
Guide Time:	4½ hours

From the T-junction ❶ in the centre of Machynlleth proceed N for 1km and over the river bridge. Turn left (W) along the A493 for 250m. Here take the metalled lane on the right, which rises quite steeply and is signposted 'Cycle Route 8'. The direction soon changes from W to NNW and rises continuously. At the end of the metalled track, pass through a gate to continue on a forest track. This is easy walking, heading NW and maintaining one contour for approximately 500m to GR SH729032 ❷.

Here, at an intersection of paths, care needs to be taken to bear left (W) and almost immediately right, leaving the main stone forest road for the lesser grassy rutted track, which rises slightly. This track heads WNW for approximately 150m before turning N. The area on your left has been deforested.

After roughly 600m on the N heading look carefully for a faint footpath on your left to allow the same bearing to be maintained. As a guide to locating this path, it begins when the track starts to descend slightly and curves away to the E (GR SH728039). Depending upon the time of year, if you look ahead (N) to the area still forested you may spot the fire notice. Continuing on the unclear footpath, pass through a gateway and past the fire notice. Continue ahead (N) through the plantation, ignoring the paths on the left, to reach the ruins of Pantyspydded. Turn left at the ruins and follow a forest track around a right-hand hairpin bend rising gently. Continue on

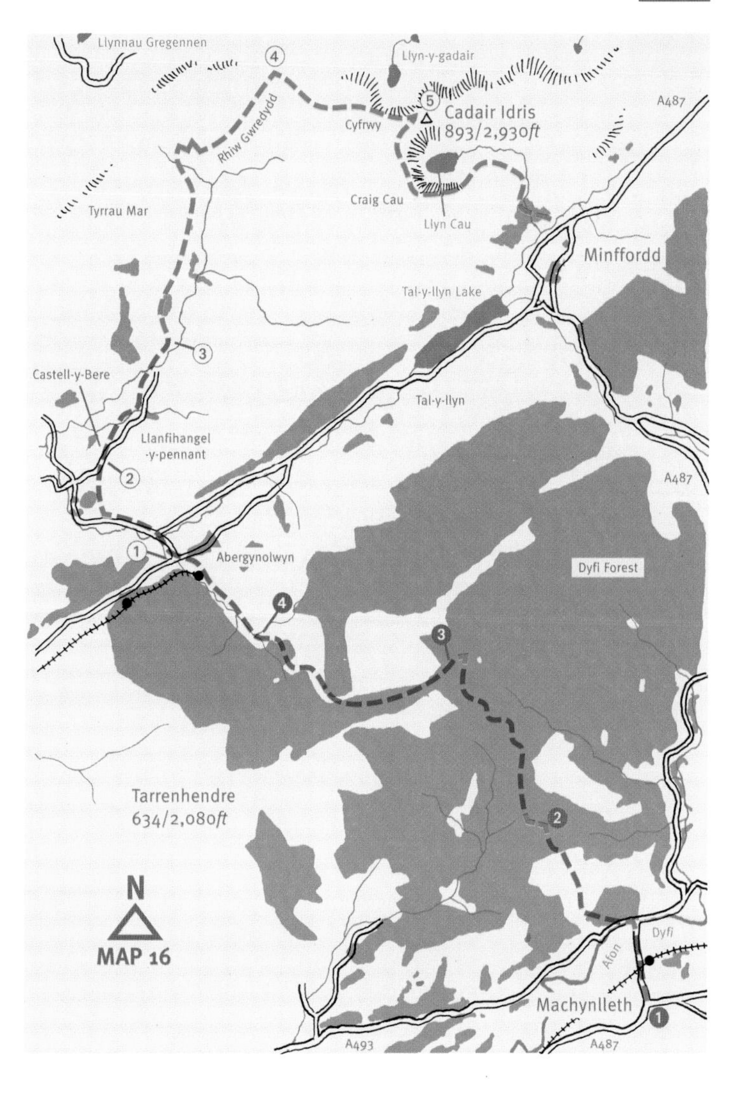

this track for approximately 1km, when the track peters out to give way to a waymarked narrow footpath heading N. Follow this for 500m to a stile and a wonderful view (weather permitting).

Do not cross the stile but turn left up a grassy bank path,

keeping the fence on your right to reach the fence corner and paths junction at GR SH717054 ❸. At this point continue ahead (initially SW) descending to cross over a bridge (Pont Laeron) heading NW to old mine workings and a disused quarry at Bryn Eglwys, before joining the unfenced vehicular lane ❹ leading down into Abergynolwyn.

Cadair Idris and Abergynolwyn

Cadair Idris is an impressive feature of the southern part of the Snowdonia National Park. At 892m (2,928ft) high it is a mighty mountain towering above the glacial U-shaped valley and Tal-y-llyn lake to the south, the Mawddach river and estuary to the north, the Dysynni Valley to the west and the high ground towards Corns and Dinas Mawddwy to the east and northeast.

The summit of Cadair Idris is called Penygadair and the views from here on a fine day are stupendous. It is said that anyone who spends a night on the mountain is fated either to wake up a poet or a madman, or perhaps not to wake up at all. Other legends abound, one of the earliest claiming that the giant Idris lived there and that three large stones resting at the foot of the mountain were sent tumbling down when he became angry and kicked them. However, another story asserts that the name translates as the 'Seat of Arthur' and King Arthur made his kingdom there. Appropriately the film *First Knight* (about Arthur, Guinevere and Lancelot) was made on location south of the mountain at Tal-y-llyn and, as the castle of Camelot, the disused nuclear power station at Trawsfynydd was dressed up in battlements to look the part.

On the approach to Cadair Idris from Abergynolwyn is Castell y Bere, an ancient fortification dating back to 1221. Unusually it was started by a Welshman, Llewellyn the Great, but the castle survived for less than a century. The remains have now been partly restored. Also on this same approach is the Mary Jones Memorial in the hamlet of Tyn-y-ddol. It commemorates her barefoot walk over the mountains to Bala in 1800, aged 16, to obtain a Welsh language bible. Above the Dysynni Valley is Craig y Aderyn (often known as the Bird Rock). This was once a sea cliff but by the 18th century had been deserted by the sea, which is now over 8km (5 miles) away. Its maritime past has not been forgotten however – successive generations of cormorants still use the crags as a breeding ground. It makes yet another easy walk from several starting points, with splendid views from the top.

The narrow gauge steam railway from Towyn to Abergynolwyn, is a reminder of the days of lead and copper mining in the area, and the old workings can be seen approaching Abergynolwyn from Machynlleth.

Section 24
Abergynolwyn to Minffordd

Distance:	14.9km (9¼ miles)
Grade:	Moderate/tough
Terrain:	Ascent and descent of Cadair Idris via quiet lanes, hill and mountainside footpaths, bridleways and tracks. Care needed, particularly at high level in bad weather. Skill with map and compass needed
Maps:	OS Explorer OL23: Cadair Idris and Bala Lake
Route Map:	Map 16; Page 73
Guide Time:	6 hours

Leave the B4405 in the centre of Abergynolwyn (1) taking the lesser road NW. After 250m the road crosses the River Dysynni by the Pont y Cwrt before rising steeply to a T-junction. Continue WNW for 380m to where the road changes direction from NW to W. Cross a stile in the right banked hedge. Follow the waymarked footpath, which winds around the hill, eventually following a stone wall after crossing a stile, going through a gate and over another stile to a farm track. Pass through the kissing gate before descending NNE to join a lane opposite Castell y Bere (2). Continue on the same heading along the road, which turns N after the chapel for approximately 700m before crossing over a river bridge. Here, turn right passing Mary Jones' cottage and follow the metalled track with the river on your right until reaching a gate, which indicates the extent of vehicle access (3).

At a second gate and information board (GR SH676106) take the footpath to the right, which rises steeply to rejoin the track at GR SH679114. Continue N along a track, changing to NW, for approximately 1km before the route heads E climbing the hillside up a zig-zag waymarked footpath.

After 200m or so the route heads off initially SE but very quickly turns NE, N and finally NNE on a well defined rising path to reach the Pony Path for Cadair Idris (4).

Turn right (SE) on the very well used Pony Path, which is ever rising over rocky/stony ground. After climbing upward for approximately 1.5km, a stone windbreak shelter will be reached and the path will have moved to an easterly direction. (Note: In bad weather and particularly in poor visibility great care needs to be exercised for the next few kilometres.)

After passing the sheltered enclosure, turn SE following the precipitous edge (not too close) high above Llyn y Gadair. The cliff-edge path turns ENE and climbs steeply up to the highest point on the Cadair Idris range at Penygadair (5) (trig point at 893m). Just past the trig point is a well maintained bothy which can be a welcome shelter in bad weather.

From the trig point at Penygadair take care to head SW to join a path which immediately divides. Take the left-hand fork SW between slab stones with numerous cairns.

After descending, the path levels out. As it starts to ascend take the left fork at GR SH709123, climbing steeply to a ladder-stile. Beware of the precipitous edge falling away to a lake on the left.

Cross the stile and follow the clear descending Minffordd Path for approximately 2km towards conifer woodland below, followed by steps down to a car park.

Castell y Bere

Section 25
Minffordd to Dinas Mawddwy

Distance:	16.9km (10½ miles)
Grade:	Moderate/tough
Terrain:	Bridleways, metalled roads, high level footpaths, areas of hillside with indistinct or non-existent paths. Care needed, particularly in bad weather
Maps:	OS Explorer OL23: Cadair Idris and Bala Lake
Route Map:	Map 17; Page 78–9
Guide Time:	6 hours

Leaving the car park at GR SH732116 ❶, turn left (NE) to a road junction. Pass the Minffordd Hotel on the left and, at GR SH737118, leave the road by a lay-by leading to a caravan park and Cwmrhwyddfor Farm. Ignore the first turning to the farm and caravan site and take the track straight ahead through a gate. The track ascends between crags with a stream to the left, crossing two gate/stiles and emerging onto the A487.

Cross the road and pass a lay-by on the left to continue to a ladder-stile on the right ❷. Following the public footpath signpost (Llwybr Cyhoeddus in Welsh), continue up ENE on a grass/scree path, which becomes steep over the occasional stream-bed to reach a col between Bwlch Llyn Bach and Cefn y Clawdd. On reaching a stone wall on the left follow this going right, over and down, heading ESE to cross a wide track followed by fords at the bottom of a boggy valley.

Leave the wall on the left to stay on the same bearing and climb on a grassy path through marsh grass. Traverse to the right of a small gully and stream (SE), then climb steeply left (E). The path becomes more distinct as the route becomes less steep before reaching a ladder-stile at the fence. Cross the stile and go left (NE) at GR SH767134 on a moorland grass track with a fence on your left for approximately 2.5km to the stone trig point of Waun-oer, which can be seen over the wire fence at GR SH786148 ❸.

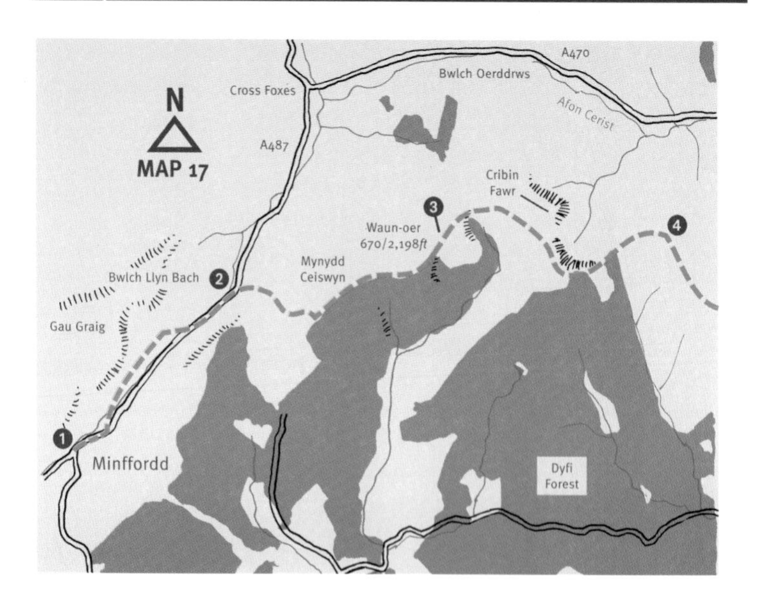

Continue ENE past a solar box station on the right, 30m from the trig point, and follow the path with the fence still to the left. Head down veering NE with a wood and looped service road down on the right. The path becomes steep here and can be slippery. Exercise great care as there is a drop on the right, which could be hazardous in misty weather.

The track snakes down to a ladder-stile at a crossing of wire fences in a gully (GR SH790151). Cross and climb up a steep bank heading ENE going right, before the crest, to join a boggy path running SSE with a wire fence approximately 30m on the left. The path improves, eventually meeting the wire fence on the left and the opportunity should be taken to cross over as there is no evidence of any stile. From the dip, climb steeply up a grass path to the crest (heading SE) to meet a wire fence.

Go left (E) and closely follow the wire fence on the right. The path skirts the precipitous feature of Craig Portas on the left. Follow a narrow grassy corridor veering left ENE (exercise care crossing the steep gully dropping away to the left). Proceed down into a dip with a wood on the right. Continue up with a wire fence right.

continued from left with overlap

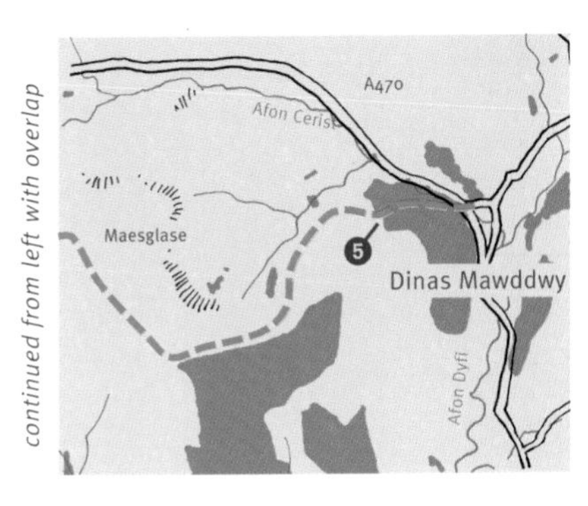

You will need to negotiate a boggy section by keeping close to a wire fence adjacent on the right. Follow it as it turns down to the left (NE) and then up to the right (ENE).

Following the wire fence on the right, continue up over marshy ground to a broken ladder-stile at GR SH817148 (655m) with Craig Rhiw-erch over to the left ❹. Cross and turn SE following a fence on the right (SE). Go down for approximately 1.7km to the conifer wood at GR SH827135. Go left (ENE) with the wire fence and wood on the right for about 1km. The path snakes down steeply via zig-zags to a ridge in a dip with a wood and Bwlch Siglen on the right and the valley of Maes-glase-bach on the left. Rejoin the wire fence on the right and follow the ridge. Take a contour path on the left-hand side at GR SH837137, heading initially NE. This is a tricky path, narrow and slippery. Proceed with caution. Continue to a ladder-stile over a wire fence, now heading N. Cross and proceed along the grass path on the side of the steeply inclined Foel Dinas.

Follow this narrow route along a contour, passing marker posts and a fenced spring on the left, exercising care in poor weather, for about 1.5km. Eventually you will drop down to a marginally better path going NE then E to meet a wood at GR SH847151 ❺. Continue with a wire fence and conifer wood to the left for 150m to reach a stile as the wire fence rises up to the right.

Cross into a rhododendron and conifer wood dropping away to the left. The path, which is initially difficult, heads down to the E, eventually improves and descends zig-zagging via waymarks to join a hardcore track. Go right for approximately 80m ESE, then left at a waymark down slab steps and along a shale path to a further zig-zag section, reaching steps to a waymarked exit onto a main road (A470) at GR SH856150. Turn right (SE) for 60m, then take the slip road on the left to Dinas Mawddwy, arriving at a T-junction at the end of the main street.

On the Minffordd Path beneath Cadair Idris

Section 26
Dinas Mawddwy to Llanuwchllyn

Distance:	18.5km (11½ miles)
Grade:	Moderate/tough
Terrain:	Quiet lanes, tracks, hill and mountainside footpaths. Paths indistinct in places, particularly in sections along the grass and rocky ridge areas of the Arans
Maps:	OS Explorer OL23: Cadair Idris and Bala Lake
Route Map:	Map 18; Page 82
Guide Time:	7½ hours

From the T-junction ❶ by the Red Lion in the centre of Dinas, take the road heading downhill signposted 'Llanymawddwy'. Continue as the road sweeps left (NNE), over a bridge over the River Dovey. After approximately 800m take the first left turn marked '2 tons weight limit'.

Ignore the immediate rising track to the left but proceed along the road, which eventually turns into a bridleway at Nant yr Henfaes ❷. After several gates and stiles you will rejoin the original road. Here turn left along the metalled road away from a bridge and river. Cross over a cattle grid and continue along the straight road to a footbridge on the right marked 'Aran Fawddwy/Aran Benllyn' ❸.

Continue NE for almost 3km, traversing NW up the side of Pen yr Allt Uchaf and Waun Goch. This path initially is hedged with shale/rock footing, then grass/peat and is fenced. Follow the waymarkers upwards, to arrive at a ladder-stile. Proceed up through marsh grass, ENE then NE to a crest at GR SH875205. Turn NNW at a stub waymark post continuing steeply up for 800m. This path is clear and follows a wire fence on the right leading to a ladder-stile at the crest of Drysgol ❹.

Follow the contour (left) heading W along the ridge for 1km, joining a wire fence on the right to arrive at a memorial cairn up on the left. Take care here in bad weather. Continue NW, then N and, at the junction of fences, turn right with an escarpment down on the right and Aran Fawddwy up ahead. The path goes NNE and undulates over rocky outcrops, with a fence to the right, and arrives at a ladder-stile. Cross and continue up over the meandering, rocky, faint path to a cairn on a NE bearing. Do not follow the wire fence going left.

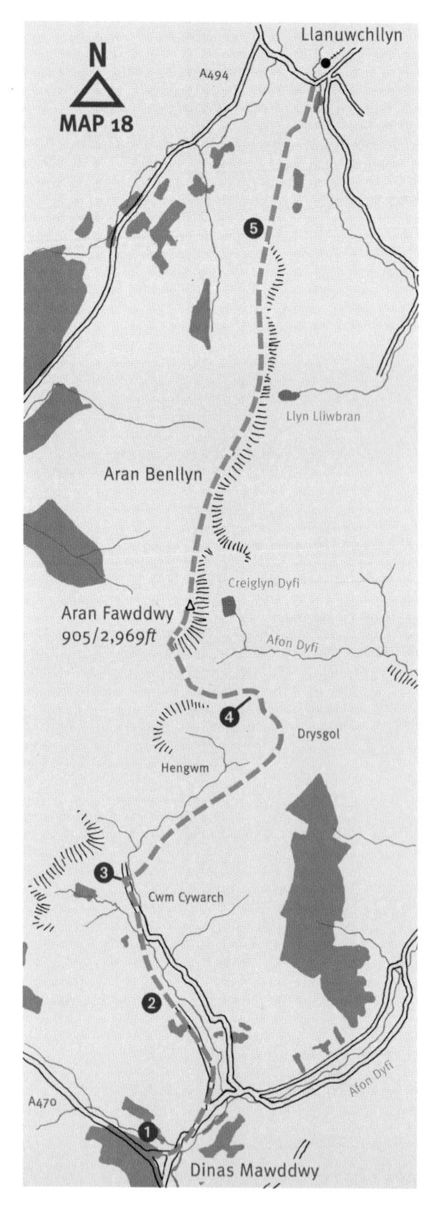

Continue down, following the fence where possible, using boards over a marshy area. Cross a ladder-stile and walk N to obtain a first view of Llyn Tegid (Bala Lake) ahead right. Reaching a further ladder-stile, follow the established path/track down over the grass/rock/peat route N through heather to reach a wire fence on the left and the next ladder-stile at GR SH873275 ❺.

The route undulates NNE, over ladder-stiles and walls, and up over a gorse strewn hill for 1km to join a grass track (ignore the stile to Peniel on the left and the ladder-stile on the right up to Garth Fawr).

The grass track veers N over fields and ladder-stiles/gates down to a bridleway. Turn right NNE and follow this track over a cattle grid as it descends to the valley of the River Twrch, heading NE with the river on the right.

Join the road at a gate/ladder-stile and go left (NW) into centre of Llanuwchllyn.

Section 27
Llanuwchllyn to Bala

Distance:	10.5km (6½ miles)
Grade:	Easy
Terrain:	Footpaths, metalled roads and quiet lanes. Some rough grassland and field walking
Maps:	OS Explorer OL23: Cadair Idris and Bala Lake
Route Map:	Map 19; Page 84
Guide Time:	3½ hours

Leave Llanuwchllyn ❶ on the B4403 heading NW. Join a footpath adjacent to the public conveniences.

Passing a house on the left, go through the yard, bearing left to a hidden stile in the wall. Bear NE across a meadow to a wooden gate and stile. Cross the field to go over a step-stile, keeping the hedge to the left and join a metalled track.

Turn left towards Dol-fach, go through the yard over a step-stile and footbridge, heading N to a step-stile and footbridge crossing the Afon Dyfrdwy. Ascend to the road and turn right, taking the second metalled road on the left at Lôn ❷.

Continue round to the right passing cottages on the left to join a waymarked path on the left. Head NW over rising marshy ground to a stile at the top of the rise. Follow the path waymarked on the left, crossing a stream and following a wire fence on the left to a nearby stile on the left. Cross, keeping the wire fence to the right, to a further waymarked stile and footbridge. Cross and follow the waymarked path over marshy ground along the edge of cut woodland to join a metalled track. Turn right through a gate and a further gate heading N over a rolling field to a stile on the far side. Follow the wire fence on the right (waymarked). Cross the footbridge and stile to a waymarked fence post and onto a gate and road (waymarked). Turn right along the road, descending to a bend with a gate to Llwyn-mawr-isaf on the left ❸.

Through the gate, head N along the road and, beyond Llwyn–mawr-isaf, go through a wooden gate on the right. Rise steeply NE following overhead wires to a stile.

Follow the wires NE through a gate on the right with farm buildings on the left (Llwyn-mawr-uchaf).

Follow the metalled and stone track in front of the farm and continue to a road. Turn right and continue to a right-hand bend in the road and a gate with a waymark on the left. Go through the gate heading NE across a field towards a conifer coppice. At the end of the coppice go left along a wire fence to a stile and waymarked footbridge. Take a NE bearing across tufty and marshy ground to a waymarked gate and Ty'n-y-rhos ❹.

Follow the wire fence (E) round to a waymarked gate with a view of the lake ahead. Head towards Moel-y-garnedd-uchaf farm, turn left (NE) before the buildings, and through a gate. Continue through a further

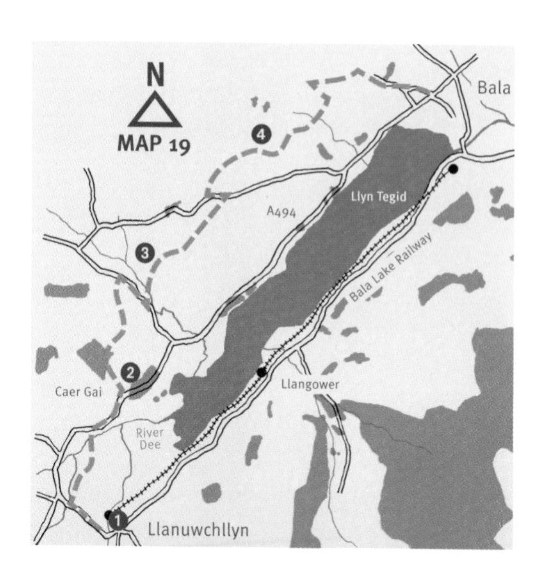

gate on the right towards a ramp and stile on the far side of the field. Pass through a caravan park and between cottages to a gate and the field beyond heading NE. Passing through a small metal gate, descend to a wooden gate and down to a hand-railed footbridge over Aber Gwenwyn-feirch. Continue, rising, across marshy ground on a NE bearing to a waymark post in the top right-hand corner of a field with two stiles, continuing to Penlan Farm.

Turn left heading NW down a metalled road past the entrance to a golf course on the right to reach a waymarked path on the left, leading to a metalled road SE. Cross the main road, pass a car park and join a waymarked path behind houses, keeping left (SE) into the town of Bala.

Bala and the Berwyns

Although in Tudor times it was considered 'a little poore market', Bala had been established as a market town since the 14th century. Prosperity only came in the 18th and 19th centuries with the hosiery and glove trade. Farming, shops and tourism now predominate. The Welsh language, which is spoken by 80 per cent of the population, is central to the lively cultural life of the town. The people of Bala are committed to the preservation of their language and culture and the town is well known for its fair-days, choirs and local agricultural shows.

Bala is set at the end of Llyn Tegid, the largest natural lake in Wales. This is the only home of the gwyniaid, a trout-like species of fish, which became trapped here during the last Ice Age. Legend has it that beneath Tegid's waters lies a drowned palace. A steam railway runs along the length of the lake. The scenery is magnificent, both town and lake being circled by the Berwyn, Aran and Arenig mountains. The nearby villages are full of character and history and the whole area offers warm hospitality to visitors.

Rising to almost 900m (2,953ft) the remote mountain range of the Berwyns is one of Wales' best kept secrets. There is a sense of freedom and escape from the world here, whether you are walking the heather-clad slopes or scaling the tree-less heights. Hidden in a fold in the range is the dramatic Lake Vyrnwy. Artificial, but ringed by mountains, this reservoir is well worth seeing. It has a startling beauty with dark waters, a Gothic tower and densely forested shores. It is the centre of a vast nature reserve, teeming with bird life.

In the foothills of the Berwyns, near Llanrhaeadr-ym-Mochnant is Pistyll Rhaeadr, the tallest waterfall in Wales. It is a breathtaking sight as the river plunges 73m (240ft) over a sheer cliff.

Section 28

Bala to Llanarmon Dyffryn Ceiriog

Distance:	31.4km (19½ miles)
Grade:	Tough
Terrain:	Metalled roads, quiet lanes, forestry tracks and footpaths. Permitted footpaths over rough grassland hillsides and the Berwyn mountain range
Maps:	OS Explorers OL23: Cadair Idris and Bala Lake and 255: Llangollen and Berwyn
Route Map:	Map 20; Page 87
Guide Time:	10 hours

Head south out of Bala ❶ to join the B4391 at the head of the lake by the car park, heading towards Llangynog. Take the first road on the right (signposted to Lake Vyrnwy) to Rhos-y-gwaliau ❷. Pass through the village to the bridge on the left and continue right, beyond the outdoor centre on a rising road over a bridge. After passing a white bungalow on the right, turn left to Gelli-Grin (SSE), through a farmyard and gate heading SE and on a stone track towards Dol-wen-uchaf. Pass through a gate and across a field (SE) to a further gate between a line of trees.

Continue on a grass track to the next gate and stone track on to Dol-wen-uchaf. Pass through a yard, continuing along a track and metalled road to Dol-wen-isaf. Continue past a yard, keeping left on the descending track to the road. Turn right and take the first ascending road on the left into a wooded area with houses on the right below.

Continue bearing left and ascending NE. At a fork turn right following a contour E, through a gate and along a stone track to Cefn-y-Meirch ❸. Go through a waymarked gate on a rising stone track to the next gate and continue through the forest. At the first junction go straight on, heading E. Take the next left fork rising to the end of the forest and a waymarked post at a turn in the track. Follow a bearing of 100 degrees to reach a marker post

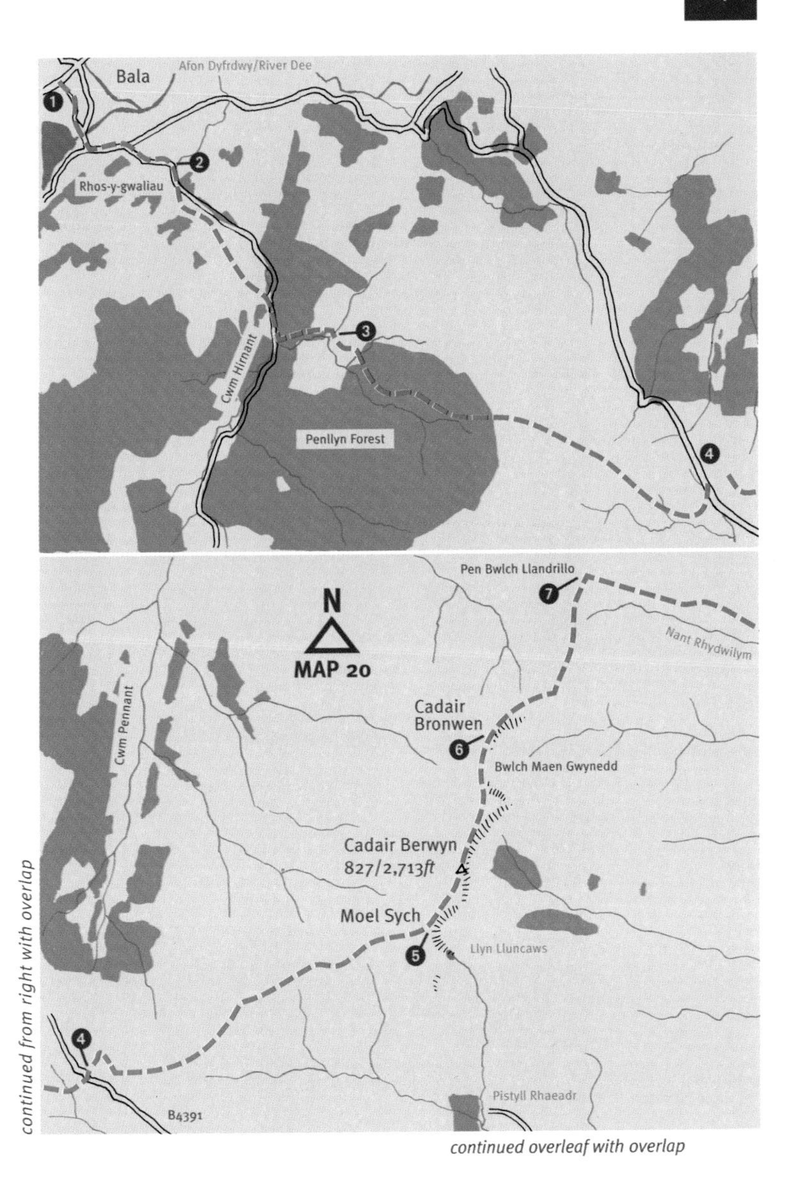

continued from right with overlap

continued overleaf with overlap

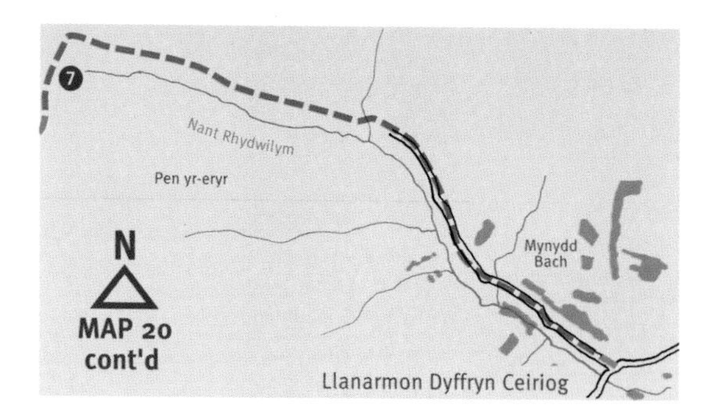

on the horizon, crossing heather covered ground.

Keep E to the next marker post then turn right on a bearing of 140 degrees to a further marker post and then follow a faint track on a bearing of 60 degrees to the next post. From there head 120 degrees down a gully. Pass a stand of conifers, cross a ford (E) up a rising stone track and through a gate. Go up the grassy waymarked track to a road (B4391) ❹.

Turn left, ascending to the stone track on the right, rising to the N (GR SJ019303). After about 150m, at a fork, keep right into the National Nature Reserve and follow the well-defined path across boggy land, at first in a SE direction but then generally NE rising to a cairn. Continue ENE still rising, to Moel Sych ❺.

At the summit cross two waymarked ladder-stiles and head NNE then N, keeping the fence on your left towards Cadair Berwyn. This is a short hard pull and great care is needed, particularly in poor visibility, with exposed crags to the right. Walk on a NE heading, following the wire fence on the left. Cross a waymarked ladder-stile and climb up NNE past a cairn to a trig point at Cadair Berwyn. Ignoring the ladder-stile on the left, continue, with good walking, NNE then NE along Craig Berwyn with a wire fence on your left for 1km.

Take the ladder-stile on the left, waymarked and heading NNW then NW, with the wire fence now on your right. Follow the fence to a corner, after approximately 100m, turn right, with the fence still on the right, down into a dip and continue up N and NE. An established path leads steeply up to a waymarked stile and the cairn of Cadair Bronwen ❻.

Follow the wire fence to the right along the lip of Craig Bronwen and over a ladder-stile down (NE). Follow the path as it continues with the fence on the right for approximately 1.5km and then, as it leaves the fence, head NNE up on a path through crags to a cairn and descend to the Memorial Stone ❼ at a track. Turn right following the track for approximately 4km, to join a lane at Swch-cae rhiw farm. Follow the lane into Llanarmon Dyffryn Ceiriog or, as an alternative, approximately 400m after joining the lane, take a footbridge across the river (NE) and follow the footpath SE into the village.

Above Bala

Section 29
Llanarmon Dyffryn Ceiriog to Llangollen

Distance:	16km (10 miles)
Grade:	Easy/moderate
Terrain:	Quiet lanes, hillside tracks, bridleway and footpaths over moorland, bracken and rough grassland
Maps:	OS Explorer 255: Llangollen and Berwyn
Route Map:	Map 21; Page 91
Guide Time:	5 hours

From the crossroads ❶ in the centre of Llanarmon DC take the road past the West Arms. Cross the river bridge and ascend the road ahead NNE at GR SJ157328. Continue on the road past a farm on the right to a white cottage. Proceed onto a

Between Llanarmon DC and Llangollen

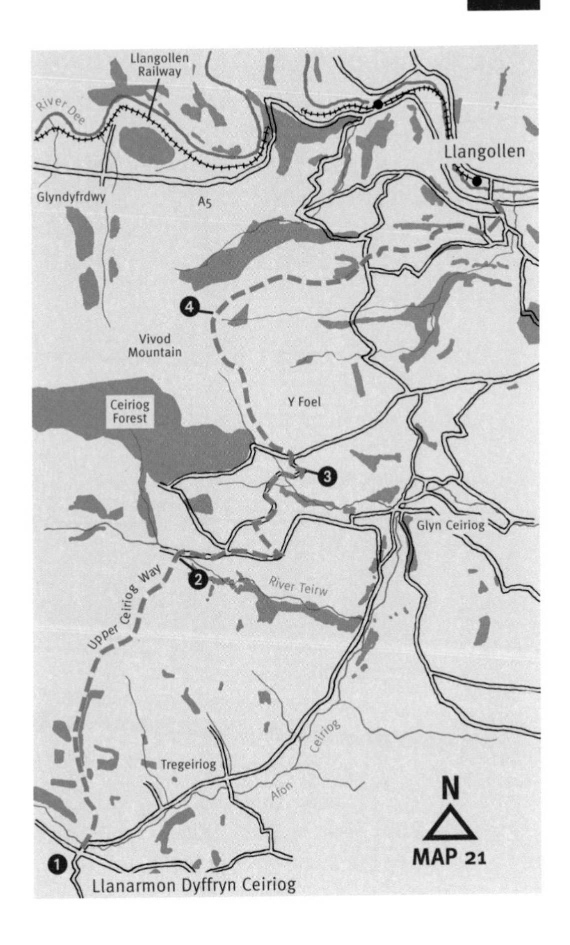

stone track heading NNW and rising, through a wooden gate, to open moorland. Continue on the rutted track joining Upper Ceiriog Way.

Follow the waymarks down to a metalled road and continue straight ahead (NNE) over another river bridge. At a telephone kiosk by a lane junction ❷ turn right by the chapel (E) to the second road junction and left towards Llangollen. Follow the road as it descends through some sharp bends to a bridge in a wooded glade with hidden waterfalls. The road then rises to a road junction at GR SJ189382 ❸.

Take the track left (NW) and continue on the same track to reach a road. Cross directly over and continue up the rutted track (NW) as it narrows to a path alongside a conifer wood on the right with a wire fence on the left.

At the end of the wood, go through a wooden gate onto open moorland on a rising path NW towards a stand of trees and a wooden gate. Go through the gate and trees, continuing on the descending rutted stone track. Reaching a crossroads in tracks at GR SJ175404 ❹, turn right. Continue along the track to a crossroads at GR SJ182408 and turn right, heading ENE and eventually E, keeping the wire fence on the right. Descend to a road, cross directly over it to join a shale track down into Llangollen (by any of the various possible obvious descents).

Llangollen

Llangollen is an ancient market town situated on the banks of the beautiful River Dee under the watchful gaze of Dinas Bran Castle. Home to the International Musical Eisteddfod, the town's population of just over 3,000 increases dramatically during the Eisteddfod week in July. The Royal International Pavilion hosts the Eisteddfod and a variety of other entertainment throughout the year.

The area abounds in legends and historic ruins, from the Iron Age and the original Dinas Bran Castle through to the early medieval period and the legendary King Arthur. The remains of the once proud Valle Crucis Cistercian Abbey were built, probably on the site of earlier buildings, around 1200 by a local Welshman, Madoc ap Gruffydd, Prince of Powys, who lived at Dinas Bran Castle.

Eliseg's Pillar is one of the most important early medieval artefacts in the whole of the British Isles. Erected by Concenn, ruler of Powys in the 9th century AD, it was to commemorate his great-grandfather Eliseg, from whom the whole valley is named and who saved Powys from falling into the hands of the Saxons.

Many of the towns other attractions are firmly rooted in its past, such as the Llangollen Wharf, Plas Newydd (the home of the famed Regency period 'Ladies of Llangollen') and the Llangollen Railway.

Langollen bridge was built in 1345 by John Trevor I, Bishop of St Asaph. The bridge was the only stone structure over the River Dee for some considerable distance in either direction. It was rebuilt in Elizabethan times and that structure remains to this day, unaltered on the lower side and perfectly copied on the upper side when it was widened in 1873. Ten years earlier the 'square arch' was added to accommodate the new railway line into the town.

Section 30
Llangollen to Froncysyllte

Distance:	8km (5 miles)
Grade:	Easy
Terrain:	Towpath of the Shropshire Union Canal
Maps:	OS Explorer 255: Llangollen and Berwyn
Route Map:	Map 22; Page 93
Guide Time:	2 hours

Leave Llangollen ❶ by crossing the bridge at the end of Castle Street (over the River Dee). Turn left onto Abbey Road and, shortly, right by a waymark, ascending via steps to the canal. Go right (E) along the towpath on the S side of the canal. The canal snakes E following the road and the Vale of Llangollen. Follow the scenic canal walk as it crosses under the A539 and continue for approximately 6km. At Cysylltan Bridge ❷ Offa's Dyke Path joins from the NW. Continue on the towpath passing the bridge at Trevor to your left. Turn right (S) along the B5434, crossing the road and, almost immediately, locate a waymark sign to rejoin Offa's Dyke Path. This will take you over the bridge, turning right to join the towpath which heads S towards, then over, the aqueduct. Continue S along the E bank of the canal and then ESE and to the north of Froncysyllte. At the B5606 ❸, leave the towpath, turning right along the road and almost immediately right again over a stile into a field heading W. Turn at a hedge (SSW) and follow it to join the main A5, 1km ESE of Froncysyllte.

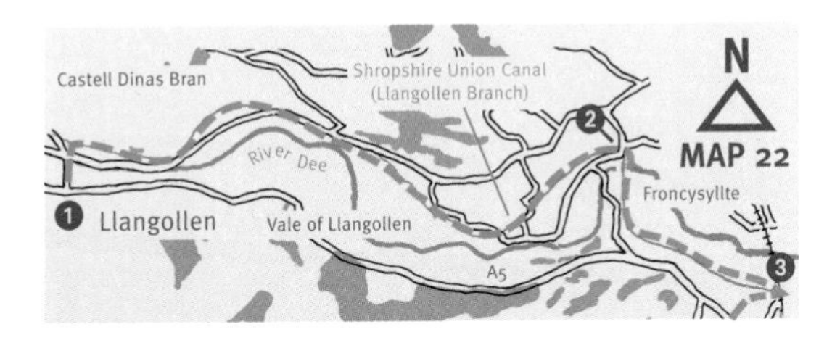

Telford's great aqueduct carries the Shropshire Union Canal

Section 31
Froncysyllte to Craignant

Distance:	8.9km (5½ miles)
Grade:	Easy
Terrain:	Quiet lanes, field and woodland footpaths and tracks
Maps:	OS Explorer 255: Llangollen and Berwyn
Route Map:	Map 23; Page 96
Guide Time:	2½ hours

This section follows the Offa's Dyke Path. Join Offa's Dyke path at Plas-Offa Farm on the A5 ❶, locating a stile in the wall just W of the farm and heading WSW over a field with a hedge left and a hill ahead. Proceed to the stile in the far left-hand corner and continue diagonally across the next field on rising ground (W) to a marker post in the top right-hand corner. Go slightly left to a waymarked stile into a lane (30m ahead). Continue S, then SW down a hedged lane (Stryt y Veri), going straight over at a crossroads, with Wern Wood on the left. Proceed up a lane past Fron cottage on the left and up to a junction. Continue SW (the Dyke runs almost parallel but 200m to the east). Shortly, come to Caeaugwynion Farm on the left, then go right at a waymarker opposite a barn. Go up the track and immediately left, over a stile into a field. Now head diagonally (SW) up to a waymarked stile in the far corner. Continue on a line of large oak trees straight ahead to find a marker, and stile under it, before exiting onto a lane.

Turn right (SW) along the lane for 750m. Walk on past Tyn-y-groes kennels on the right and Pool Wood on the left. Soon the road turns acutely right and, further around the bend on the left, just beyond a stone cottage, take the waymarked stile into a field and head SW, up a rise past a large oak tree on the left to a gate and stile. Continue straight over the next field (SW) to a further stile on a crest, with Mars Wood on the left and Warren Wood, right.

Cross a field to a gate and stile and drop steeply down SW, with woods right and left and hills ahead, to find a marker post at the end of a wall. Proceed down to a stile to the right of a metal gate, emerging onto a track. Go left (SSE) down the track past buildings on the right and left and, 250m ahead, an old yew tree on the left.

Continue down to arrive at Ty Brickly on the right, then go left up along the lane (ESE) and down to emerge onto a road (B4500) opposite Castle Mill ❷. With care, cross straight over (S) and continue up over a stone bridge over the River Ceiriog.

The road goes left then right rising steeply up to a T-junction at Pen-y-bryn. Cross straight over to a path up between houses and, at the top, turn left and proceed up a hedged path, with a disused quarry and Bronygarth to the left, to join a track. Continue right to a double stile and up over a field to a marker post (SW). Walk steeply uphill, crossing a series of stiles, over a green lane and up on to the Dyke itself. Offa's Dyke forms the county boundary here and the border between England and Wales.

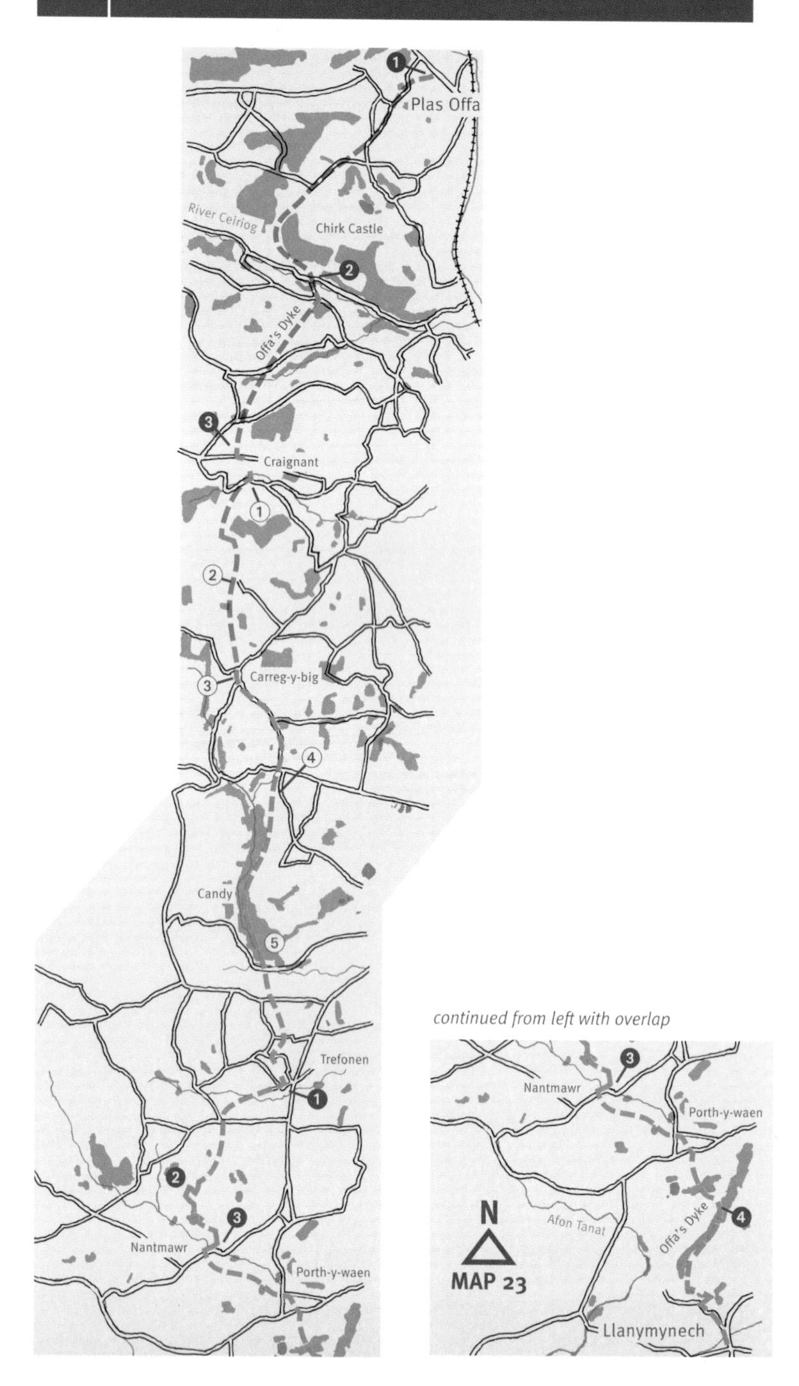
Plas Offa
River Ceiriog
Chirk Castle
Offa's Dyke
Craignant
Carreg-y-big
Candy
Trefonen
Nantmawr
Porth-y-waen
continued from left with overlap
Nantmawr
Porth-y-waen
Afon Tanat
Offa's Dyke
Llanymynech
N
MAP 23

Cross the stiles and proceed, first along the top, and then on the left-hand edge of the Dyke, with a wire fence on your left. Climb the double stiles crossing a lane and continue down a steep field to Nanteris ravine. Cross the stile to steps and a footbridge over a stream to reach more steps, which rise steeply up the far side into a field, with a hedge and the Dyke on the right.

Continue SSW to a double stile and walk along the gorse-covered Dyke over open moorland. Proceed to a further double stile over a lane, with Mount Wood to the E and Plas-crogen to the W. Continue straight down to a stile onto a lane ❸. Go left (E) along the lane for approximately 70m and turn right (SSE) past the entrance to a house and take the next exit down a green lane, leading to a metalled track past Yew Tree farmhouse on the right.

Continue, following the metalled road, turning right and left going down, bearing left and crossing a stream (Thornhill on the right). Continue easterly with a stream on your left-hand side and up to a T-junction on the B4579.

Section 32
Craignant to Trefonen

Distance:	8.9km (5½ miles)
Grade:	Easy/moderate
Terrain:	Metalled roads, field and woodland footpaths, quiet lanes and tracks
Maps:	OS Explorer 240: Oswestry
Route Map:	Map 23; Page 96
Guide Time:	2½ hours

From the junction in Craignant ① take the rising grassy metalled lane at GR SJ255350, heading WSW, then SSW with a ridge falling away to the right.

After the gate with a waymarked stile, continue straight on where the track heads left, to join a further low walled and hedged track up to a marker post and onto a crest. The walled track continues to a gate and stile into a field where, noting the marker post at an outstanding corner on the left, you should proceed SSE, turning E to a stile at the corner of a fir wood. Go right (SSE) with a fence on the right (care is needed here) before proceeding down to a gate and waymarked stile onto a further hedged track, leading to two more gate/stiles and up to a marker post.

Go right (W) onto a track by Orseddwen Farm ② and, after 30m, cross a cattle grid. Go left at a marker post to a waymarked stile in a wire fence. After 20m enter a field with a stone wall and hedge on the right and walk down the steep gully. Cross a wooden footbridge over a stream, to go up over the bank with steps/stile to arrive back on the Dyke heading S, with Brook Cottage on the left.

With the Dyke on the right, walk S to a stile and proceed (with a small wood to your right) over a field to a stile at the edge of a further small wood on the left, with a fence and field to the right. This emerges into a gorse field with marsh grass and a wire fence, right. Continue S into a dip with a cross track (ignore the stile to the right). Cross the plank bridge over a stream and walk over a marshy field to the next stile, then continue straight on to a stile waymarked 'Chepstow 127 miles' on one side and 'Prestatyn 49 miles' on the reverse.

Go right (W) onto the road at Carreg-y-big ③, passing farm buildings on the left to a T-junction. Take the road left (SE) to the reach the B4580, which rises adjacent to Baker's Hill, by the old racecourse. Continue to a broken cross roads and cross the B4580 left then right, onto a grassy verge with a small pool on the right.

Continue S over a grassy common alongside the road and, keeping right at a fork in the track ④ (SSW) as you leave the road, pass a picnic site on the left and Grandstand Cottage on the right. There are plaques here erected by the Rotary Club of Oswestry with a topograph and views of the west and south. Proceed to the right of a stone horse's saddle seat sculpture to a waymarked stile into Racecourse Wood. Go down to exit over a stile with a fence on the left and scrub on the right. Continue into an overgrown dip, with a marker to the left, and into the wooded area. Note with care the second marker to the right. Go right here, then left, with a wall and bank on the left (SSW) and a wooded ridge and valley down on the right.

This is a very pleasant level section, which then goes down to a narrow fork. Take the right-hand path at a waymark, down, past rocky outcrops on the left.

Skirt round, passing stone seats constructed in the rocks on the left and walk down to a waymarker post, turning right at the crossing of tracks. Soon turn left (SW) to a further crossing track and go left at a marker post down to join an overgrown path, emerging at a track adjacent to a stone house.

Continue S along the hardcore track to a T-junction, with a white stone cottage on the left. Go right along the lane and shortly cross a bridge over the Morda at Tyn-y-coed ⑤, past the Old Mill Inn on the left.

Walk left past the inn on the right then proceed left before turning steeply right up the road to a T-junction, with Pentre-shannel to the right. Go left at a junction then soon right at a waymarked stile into a field, with a hedge on the right, to rejoin the Dyke, crowned in trees in this overgrown section. Cross a stile at the top then turn right, off the Dyke (SSE) with a hedge on the left, to a waymarked stile in the far corner of the field and out into a lane.

Go left then right over a waymarked stile and gate into a field with a hedge on the left, and continue down to a marker post, but do not cross the stile. Turn right, with a fence left, then cross to the waymark on a railway sleeper and onto a stile. Cross (S) over the lane onto a waymarked track with the stone wall of Fron Farm on the right and a field to the left.

Proceed SSE, past a white cottage on the right, and onto a grass track to a single wooden gate leading to a hedged path. There are modern housing developments either side of the path before you emerge onto Malthouse Close (Trefonen).

Section 33
Trefonen to Llanymynech

Distance:	8.9km (5½ miles)
Grade:	Easy/moderate
Terrain:	Footpaths, tracks and lanes, some steep sections
Maps:	OS Explorer 240: Oswestry
Route Map:	Map 23; Page 96
Guide Time:	2½ hours

From Malthouse Close ❶ in Trefonen proceed along Malthouse Lane to a T-junction, with the Old Malthouse on the left, then go right (WSW), ignoring the footpath to the left. Go along Bellan Lane and keep straight on, as the lane goes right, along a track to a gate/stile.

Enter a field and pass to the left of the hedge (WSW) down to a stile to cross a stone-slab bridge over a stream. Take the stile into the next field, with a hedge to the left and a stand of trees to the SW. Cross the stile and walk up over an open field, following the line of two large trees to a waymarked stile onto a lane, with Trefonen Hall to the right.

Go left along a lane, then right at a junction on a metalled track passing Ty-Canol Farm on the right. A metalled track skirts to the left of the farmyard as you continue S, with a rocky limestone ridge and trees on the left and a fence and fields, right. Walk along the track into a dip and go right at a waymarked gate into a field, with a hedge to the right, to proceed (WSW) up to the right-hand corner. Go left, with a hedge on the right, at Moelydd Uchaf ❷ (SSE). Go slightly right at the hedge corner by a marker post.

Continue up the rocky track to a gate/stile. Go right here, up a track then left up the rutted section, leaving the track at a marker post. Go acutely left at the top via two marker posts, heading S, down to a track with a rock and scree-lined bank on the left. Pass a waymarker post on the right and carry straight on to leave the track, following a wall/fence on the right, to a second marker post.

Turn right at the hedge corner onto an overgrown path, then follow the hedge (right) down to a stile. Continue over a scrub field to a waymarker post, going left, down to a stile into Jones's Rough.

Proceed, down a series of wooden steps and shuttered paths, onto a track going ESE with a stone cottage on the left. Keep straight on up a metalled track and go right at a waymarker post, stile and steps. Go steeply down a field towards Nantmawr, to join a hedge on the left. Halfway down the hedge take the waymarked stile on the left and traverse diagonally down across a field (SE) to a hidden stile in the corner by the side of a cream-painted house.

Continue down the overgrown, narrow path to the road ❸ and turn right, with a phone box to the left. Pass Cambrian House and the Old Manse on the right, and the Four Gables B&B on the left. Enter a dip in the road over a bridge, walk up and, watching carefully for the stile on the left (opposite a T-junction on the right), enter a woody area, climbing up to a stile on the right into a field. Cross diagonally S, up to a gate/stile at Cefn Farm and enter a lane. Turn left and walk down the valley along Cefn Lane past Cefn Lane Farm on the right.

Cross the course of a dismantled railway and continue over the crossroads to Porth-y-waen. Keep going straight up, past a junction from the left and, shortly, watch carefully for a waymarked stile on the right between two bungalows. Take the grassy fenced path down to a stile into a field with a hedge on the left. Leave the corner heading SSE to cross a stile into a track and, immediately, dogleg over the main road (A495). Go left then right along the metalled track opposite.

Continue S and, shortly, go left just beyond an oak tree on the right. Cross a field with a hedge on the right and go right at the corner to a stile opposite (S). Cross the footbridge and further double stiles over the old railway into a field.

Continue to the gap in the right corner and ascend with a hedge right, to a gate/stile to the track leading up to Jones's Coppice (SE). Continue up the hardcore track and go left at a waymark post to a gate/stile, passing onto a hedged track into a field, turning right after 50m over a waymarked stile.

Traverse left up the field to a stile (SE) at Pen-y-coed. Enter Blodwel Rock Wood, going steeply up steps and zig-zagging up to the top of a ridge ❹. On reaching the top go acutely right (SW) and continue on the undulating path along the edge of the ridge, following marker posts, to emerge adjacent to a golf course. Follow the wood path on the right of the fairway then go left and up to the right, straight past a four-way marker to a single wooden gate.

Walk on, with limestone outcrops to the left and views on the right, keeping straight on following markers and passing Asterley Rocks and a disused quarry. Turn right and descend down a loose rocky path. Turn right at the bottom onto a level path leading to a stile and further path, with a fence on the left, descending to a track. Continue down left and left again at a waymark opposite a post box and go straight down, past a coach house on the right, into Llanymynech.

Section 34
Llanymynech to Four Crosses

Distance:	4km (2½ miles)
Grade:	Easy
Terrain:	Flat walking along metalled roads and canal towpath
Maps:	OS Explorer 240: Oswestry
Route Map:	Map 24; Page 103
Guide Time:	1 hour

Depart Llanymynech from the crossroads ❶ in the centre of the village heading WSW along the B4398. Turn right after approximately 400m at Carreghofa Lane and then immediately left on the same heading. Cross a stile and go under a bridge following the towpath of the Montgomery Canal, with the canal on your right. The canal runs adjacent to the road. Proceed under two bridges, with fields on the right, to arrive at Carreghofa Toll House with its double lock and

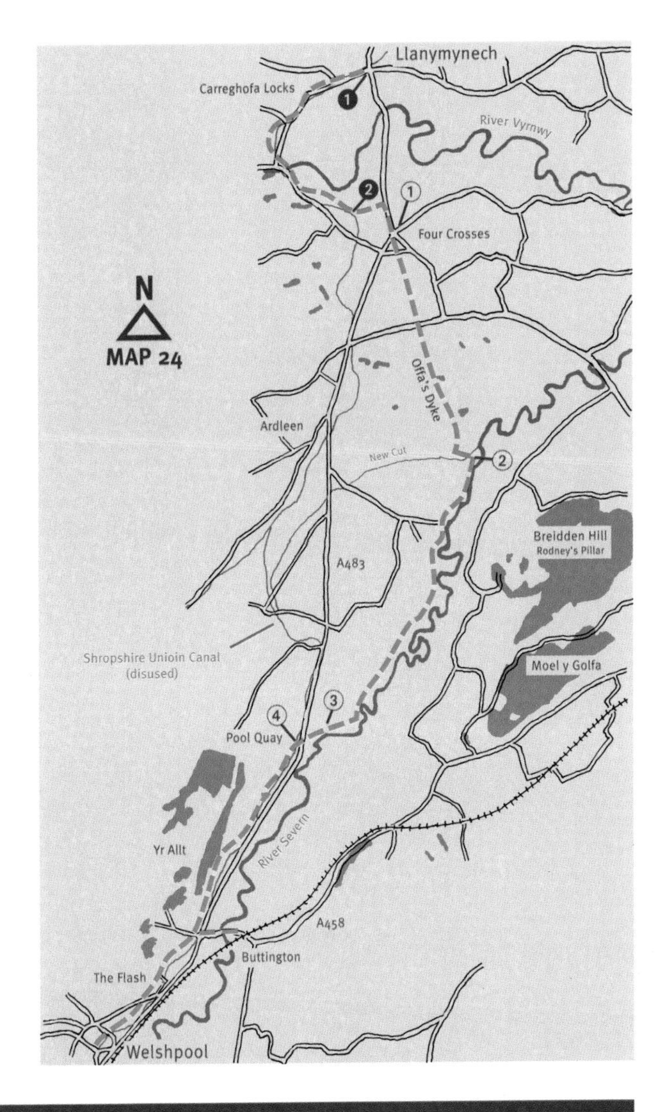

bridge. Shortly the canal leaves the road and heads out into open country.

Cross the road via two waymarked stiles and continue to follow the canal and aqueduct over the River Vyrnwy. The route follows the canal as it turns left heading ESE under a white-railed bridge and on to a second bridge. At the near side of bridge No 99 ❷, by a waymarker post, leave the canal by turning left (ENE) along Parson's Lane with Pont-y-Person farm on your right-hand side.

At the end of the lane you will emerge at a T-junction with the A483. Turn right (SSE) and walk into Four Crosses, passing the Golden Lion on the right.

Section 35
Four Crosses to Welshpool

Distance:	14.5km (9 miles)
Grade:	Easy
Terrain:	Footpaths over open fields and alongside the River Severn. Short metalled road sections and canal towpath. Mainly flat walking
Maps:	OS Explorers 240: Oswestry and 216: Welshpool and Montgomery
Route Map:	Map 24; Page 103
Guide Time:	4½ hours

From the Golden Lion ①, go past Street Cottage and Street House, turn left at the T-junction and, almost immediately, cross the road to a waymarked stile in a hedge. Cross the stile into a small field, with a hedge on the right, to the next stile. Cross straight over the road to a waymarker post and the Old Creamery Café and Takeaway on the left. Continue straight on (SSE) across a small industrial estate and locate a waymarker post on the right. Head SSE to some steps and, crossing the waymarked stile opposite them, go right along a hedged/fenced track to a gate and stile (there is a dismantled railway to the right). Enter a field with a hedge right and cross SSE onto a hedged/fenced track with a stile and with Gornel Farm on the left.

Go through the farmyard and bear right through gates then straight on following an arrow on the side of a farm building, leading up a concrete track with a building on the left and a hedge right. Proceed to a hedged/fenced track and, at a gate, continue through a field. Keep the hedge on the right to reach a waymarked stile into an open field, with an avenue of trees on either side of the grass-covered mound of Offa's Dyke. Rhos Farm is on the left-hand side and School Brook Bridge is on the right.

Follow the Dyke to two waymarked stiles crossing a road (B4393). Continue on the same heading (SSE) to a waymarked stile on the Dyke (lined by oak trees) then a marker post, keeping straight ahead. Go under the power lines with a stream on the right. Proceed on the same bearing to a waymarked stile and another in the left far corner of the field, then into Trederwen Lane. Go right and immediately left at The Nea.

Continue along the track to the left of this stone-built cottage to a metal and then a wooden gate and pass on to a hedged, grass track up to a stile. Continue along the Dyke with trees right and left and heading SSE.

Cross the next stile, with a hedge to the left, and then a further stile with a hedge now on the right. After approximately 70m go right, down to a footbridge over Bele Brook ②. Here you will join the Severn Way. Cross a field (SSW) to a bridge. Pass through double gates and go left over Derwas Bridge, which crosses the New Cut (a watercourse); at this point the Dyke meets the flood embankment of the brook.

At the far side of the bridge take the left-hand stile and proceed due E, then bear right over a flood control gate and due S to a stile.

The path now follows a flood embankment and the meandering River Severn, heading SSW for approximately 4km. Eventually, the route arrives at a gate/stile leading over the dismantled railway ③ to a further stile, with the river on the left. Continue W under power lines and down, left to a footbridge over a stream, then diagonally left (SW) to two waymarked stiles with a farm ahead. Cross a stile and go straight over the A483 (at Pool Quay) and proceed left (SSW). Shortly, watch for a waymarker on the right to go acutely right (NNW) up a lane to Top Lock ④. Bear acute left (SSW) past stone buildings on the left to join the Montgomery Canal (a branch of the Shropshire Union Canal). Continue along the bank with the canal to the right (Offa's Dyke Path is now joined with the Severn Way) and after approximately 1km arrive at a lift bridge adjacent to the A483 on the left. Continue along the towpath (now following part of the Severn Way path) with Offa's Dyke Path running adjacent to the A483. This towpath takes you into the centre of Welshpool.

Section 36
Welshpool to Montgomery

Distance:	15.3km (9½ miles)
Grade:	Moderate
Terrain:	Some steep hillside and woodland footpaths, metalled roads and quiet lanes, bridleways and canal towpaths
Maps:	OS Explorer 216: Welshpool and Montgomery
Route Map:	Map 25; Page 109
Guide Time:	6 hours

If you have walked the previous section you will need to retrace your steps from the centre of Welshpool ❶ along the towpath and, on reaching the roundabout at Buttington Cross ❷, turn right along the A485 for a short distance to Buttington Bridge.

From the bridge locate the waymark to rejoin Offa's Dyke Path turning right (SE). Go over a stile/steps (SSE) into a field and over further stiles, crossing a railway to a field and quaint footbridge over a stream. Head ESE over a further footbridge and fields to join a road (B4388). Turn right (S) at a waymarker post and cross the road past a business park. Go left at School House, through a wooden gate and up a hedged green lane with a stream on the left. Shortly, go right at a waymarker post over a stile/gate, then cut across a field (SSE) under power lines, with a hill ahead, to a further stile/gate. Go diagonally up and across a field to a stile in the far left corner.

Cross the stile and stone footbridge over a stream and go left with a hedge on the left (ESE) up to a stile/gate at the top left corner of a field. Continue up to Stone House Farm. Do not go through the farmyard but head to the right of buildings to a marker post and a stile and then left, up past a barn on the left, and outside a post, at the corner.

Continue up (SSE) on a farm drive, through a gate with a black and white cottage on the right. Go left over a stile by the cottage and across a small field to a waymarker post, taking you left over another stile.

A steep climb leads to a stile in the top right corner of a field and onto a lane waymarked 'Glyndwr's Way' on the right. Continue ENE along the lane. After approximately 80m, at a waymarker, go right up steps to a stile and proceed steeply up the fields of Buttington.

At the crest, take the stile onto a farm track. Continue straight on, then right, up a hedged track with a house and barn to the right, to reach a waymarked stile/gate. At this point go left up the field with a hedge on the left, heading ESE, steeply up to a stile in the top left corner.

Continue, going right (S) to a stile, then left with a hedge on your left (SE) to a further stile. Walk to a stile/gate and go right (SSE), diagonally across a field up towards the left edge of Cwmdingle Plantation. (Note the single marker post in the field, but do not drop right into the dingle.)

Enter the plantation at a waymarked stile and, shortly, head left at a marker (SE), then right at a second waymarker (SSW). Go straight ahead with a mast ahead and fence left. Skirt just inside the wood to a

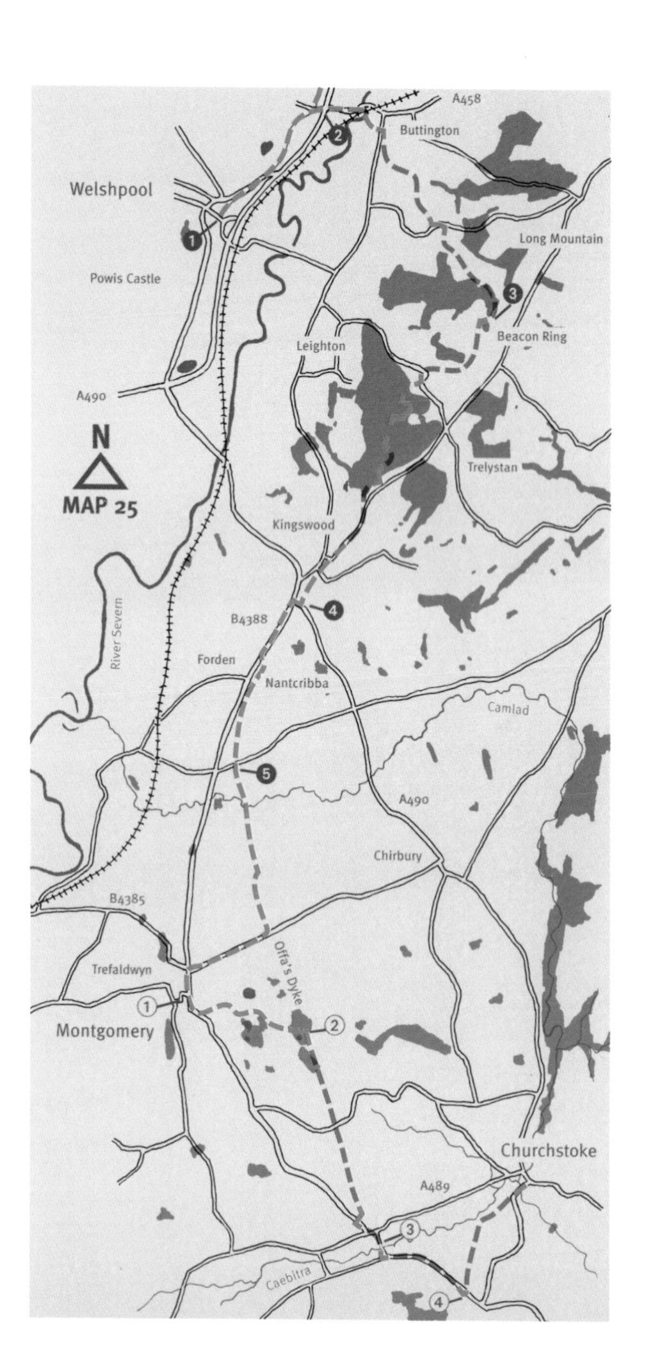
A458
Buttington
Welshpool
Long Mountain
Powis Castle
Beacon Ring
Leighton
A490
N
MAP 25
Trelystan
Kingswood
B4388
River Severn
Forden
Nantcribba
Camlad
A490
Chirbury
B4385
Offa's Dyke
Trefaldwyn
Montgomery
Churchstoke
A489
Caebitra

Raising steam in Welshpool

waymarked stile to arrive at the ancient hill fort of Beacon Ring ❸. Proceed around the earth works to the right until you reach the far side and continue down, heading SW. At the left-hand edge of Phillips Gorse, cross the stile into a wood and, at the far end of the wood, go right, along the fenced wood edge down the valley.

Take the wooden gate/stile onto a track and continue steeply down the metalled track to meet a lane and marker post opposite buildings at Pant-y-bwch. Go acutely left (SE) and, after approximately 70m, on a right-hand bend, take the stile on the right to continue down, with a wire fence on the right, into a sparse wood and on down to a pool.

Skirt left to a marker post and keep straight (SW, then W) with Roundabout Plantation up on the left. This area is part of Leighton Park. Go round, S then SE, to skirt Offa's Pool on the right. Walk first WNW then

S along Rabbit Bank. Shortly, go left up steps into a wood and continue over the crest, heading WSW, gradually down, then left up the bank at a marker post (care is needed here). This leads onto a track with a marker post. Go right, down SSW and continue left at a T-junction of tracks. Do not go down, but continue on to arrive at The Stub and then go round to the right (SW) and take the right-hand fork down a track with a rock bank on the left. There are woods and rhododendrons here to your right and left.

Shortly you will arrive at the stone-built Greenwood Lodge on the left with a cattle grid ahead. Go over the grid and turn right at the marker post to join a lane running SW, on the course of a Roman road. Continue down past the Court House on the left and, at a right-hand bend, look carefully for the waymarked stile on the left.

Cross and continue SSW, with a hedge on the right, to a stile. Follow the Dyke in a field to a further stile onto a hedged path with a kerb on the right. This emerges onto a track leading to a T-junction with a lane. Turn left and immediately right, up a bank to a waymarked stile. Follow the Dyke SW over several fields to a T-junction (by a house and shed) with the A490 ❹.

Go right and, shortly at the junction with the B4388, turn left (SW). Continue along the road for approximately 1km.

Carefully locate a left turn up a metalled drive to Nantcribba and then shortly go right, over a waymarked stile with a hedge on the left. Go straight on in line with a marker post to a stile, noting the red-brick hall on the left. Proceed SW along the Dyke, now marked with mature oak trees, passing St Michael's Church and Forden on the right with Montgomery ahead of you. Drop down and cross the lane at GR SJ232007, to continue straight up over fields with a hedge on the right and over a number of stiles with the hedge now on the left.

Go left at the crest and drop steeply down over a field to a wire fence/stile and shortly cross over two further stiles onto a road ❺. Continue SSE straight over onto a hedged track, past the Pound House on the right to a gate. Proceed straight ahead, with the hedge to the right, and locate a stile in a hedge. Cross it, then turn left to a footbridge over the River Camlad. Continue SSE over the flood bank to a wooden gate on the far left and then into a hedged/fenced track past the ruins of the red-brick Rownal Cottages on the right. Pass through further gates and up a field to Rownal Farm. Cross a stile and turn right down the track, shortly locating a wooden gate on the left to rejoin Offa's Dyke on the right.

Soon cross the Dyke at a marker post and keep on the same heading past Rownal Covert on the left. Continue over fields to reach the B4386. Turn right and follow the road into Montgomery.

Section 37

Montgomery to Churchstoke

Distance:	8.5km (5¼ miles)
Grade:	Easy
Terrain:	Relatively flat walking on metalled roads, footpaths and tracks over fields and farmland
Maps:	OS Explorer 216: Welshpool and Montgomery
Route Map:	Map 25; Page 109
Guide Time:	2 hours

Depart from the town hall (1) heading E, down Broad Street to the junction with Bishop's Castle Street and turn right. Head S with terraced houses on the left, turning left just past the children's playground into a car park. At the far end go left along a grass path and through a single wooden gate to the ENE. Turn immediately right over a railed wooden footbridge over a stream. Go left heading in the same direction and cross a field with a hedge on the left, pass through the next single wooden gate, still with the hedge on the left to a third wooden gate. Here turn right along a metalled track (SE) into Lymore Park.

Follow the track, with Upper Pool on the right and Lower Pool on the left. Continue ESE, past a cricket ground on the left, to reach a cattle grid where Offa's Dyke crosses as indicated by the acorn symbol (2).

Turn right over a stile to join Offa's Dyke Path and continue bearing SSE, passing Lower Gwarthlow on the left and Pen-y-bryn Hall on the right. Shortly pass Little Brompton Farm on the right before entering to the right of The Ditches. Keep straight on to Brompton Hall and go right, through a metal gate to a road (the B4385), turn left and, at the crossroads with the A489, go directly over with the Bluebell Hotel on the left. Continue on the road over Brompton Bridge (3) and turn left, still on the B4385. Do not enter Mellington Hall. Leaving Offa's Dyke, continue along the road passing Mellington Hall up on the right until you reach Court House Cottage (4).

Opposite Court House Cottage go left through a gate and cross the field diagonally, heading N to a stile by an oak tree. Continue N then NE over a field to a crossing over a stream with a hedge on the left (Lower Mellington Farm is on the left). Continuing on the same heading, pass through a metal gate in the right hedge of the field and straight on to pass diagonally across the next field to a gate in the top hedge.

After approximately 50m into the next field head right (NE) and continue towards the church tower, shortly reaching a cemetery hedge between two ponds. Cross the stile on your right onto a lane leading into Churchstoke.

Section 38
Churchstoke to Tankerville

Distance:	12.7km (7¾ miles)
Grade:	Easy
Terrain:	Footpaths, bridleways and tracks over hills, common and farmland. Some short sections of road walking
Maps:	OS Explorer 216: Welshpool and Montgomery
Route Map:	Map 26; Page 114
Guide Time:	3½ hours

Leaving Churchstoke ❶ go up past St Nicholas's Church with the Court House pub on the left. At the junction with the main road (A489) go right and, after approximately 200m, cross with care into Hall Bank.

Follow this lane for approximately 2km, passing Blue Barn and The Brynkin along the way, to reach a junction at Oak Cottage (GR SO288952). Cross a waymarked stile ahead and go immediately left bearing NE. Traverse on this heading to high ground and, via a stile to the left of a dip, to reach a track at Cowlton Cottage.

Follow the track heading NNE for approximately 2km, passing a fir wood on the right with Corndon Hill up on the right, behind. At the near edge of the wood note the disturbed tumulus before continuing N down the track to the road. Carry on N briefly on a lane, before crossing a cattle grid onto Stapeley Common ❷.

Head NE to Mitchell's Fold stone circle. After the stone circle and passing a building in trees on the right-hand side, continue NE, following the waymarked Stapeley Trail. Continue along this wide waymarked grassy byway with Stapeley Hill Ridge on the right. At GR SO311990 ❸, leave the main track and head ENE on an indistinct path. The route ascends Stapeley Hill and passes between the two spot height cairns. Continue on the same bearing before descending to reach a post-and-wire fence at the top of a gully. Turn left down a clear but rough track with a fence on the right. From the bottom of the gully, at a marker post, head on the same bearing across rough marshy ground, to locate a stile on the edge of a plantation. Cross over the stile and pass through the plantation to arrive at a further fence and stile.

Continue ahead (ENE) with a ditch and fence on the left and, at the end of the field, go through three gates onto the A488 at Holly Bank Cottage 4 (marked as Holly Cottage on OS Explorer 216).

Cross carefully over and take the right turn signposted to The Bog, Shelve and Pennerley. Continue straight on and up (SE) to enter Shelve Wood. Turn immediately left (NE) on a rising track in a fir wood, eventually reaching the old Roman Gravels Mine on the left. Take the short track directly opposite the Roman Gravels Mine to a gate into a field and turn right, with a post-and-wire fence on the right, and continue SE.

Leaving the fence, but still heading SE, go over a field with stone outcrops and proceed down, with small copses right and left, to a stile on the right. Just beyond a stone house in the right-hand corner, beside a gate, traverse the wooden rails and head ESE, descending a

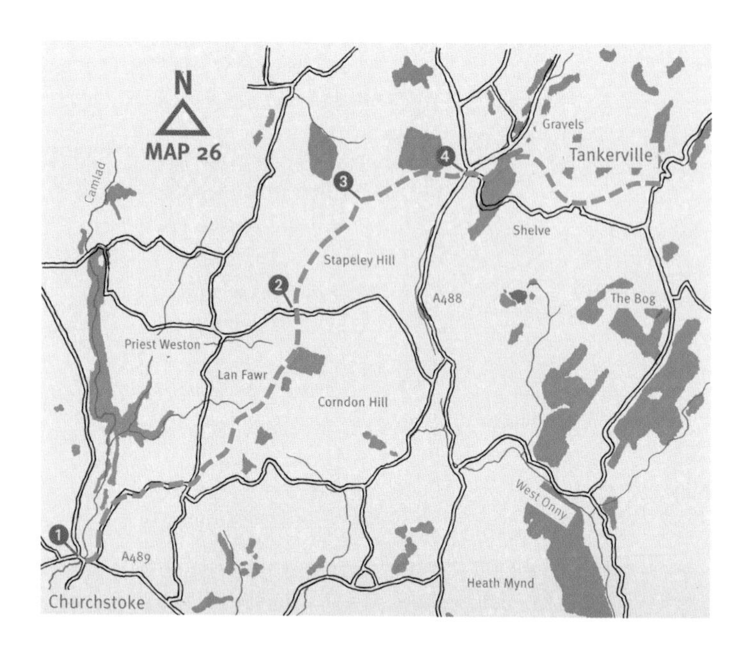

The Court House Hotel in Churchstoke

field to a gate in the far right corner. Go through the gate and head ENE over the field to a stile on the left and, on the same heading, towards a tumulus. Go over the stile beside a gate and onto a fence corner around the tumulus. Enjoy the view ahead, then skirt round the tumulus, with the fence on the right and continue to a stile with The Napp now on the right. Keeping Tankerville on the left, head E down through an enclosed, overgrown, hedged track, crossing four stiles.

After the fourth stile turn immediately right to join a road with and old mine and spring down on the left. Tankerville is now on your left at the bottom of the hill.

Section 39
Tankerville to All Stretton

Distance:	14km (8¾ miles)
Grade:	Moderate
Terrain:	Quiet lanes, tracks, bridleways and footpaths over some steep hills, rough grassland, farmland and common
Maps:	OS Explorer 217: The Long Mynd and Wenlock Edge
Route Map:	Map 27; Page 116
Guide Time:	5 hours

Leave Tankerville ❶ on a rising road heading S. After approximately 250m, take the waymarked bridle path on the left. Continue up on a steep track to Pennerley Methodist Chapel to join another track and continue left up past Rowan Trees House and Little Acres on the left. Proceed straight up a hardcore track to a gate and then on to Stiperstones, passing Pennerley Water Tank on the left.

Continue ENE along the top of the ridge with Perkins Beach on the left and Devil's Chair up on the right. On the same bearing continue over two crossing paths with Shepherd's Rock on the left to continue down to a

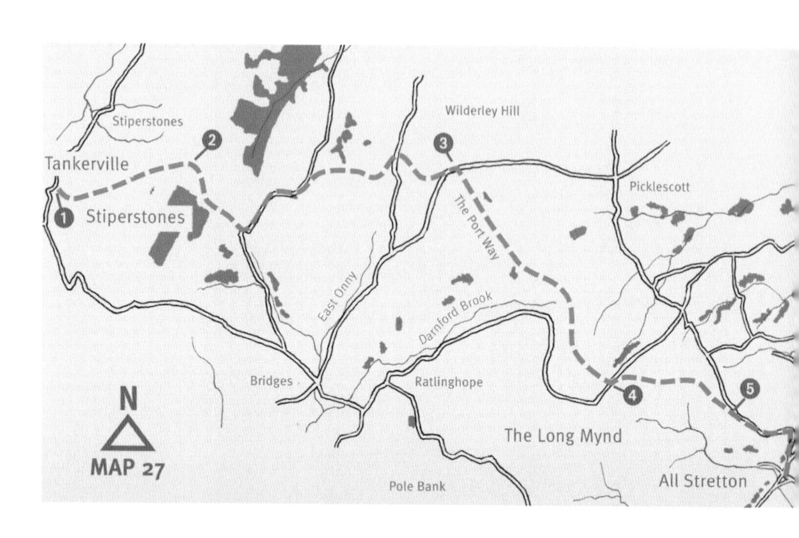

waymarked stile, marking the Shropshire Way ②. Head SSE down to The Hollies and continue SE, now along a metalled track to the road opposite a disused quarry. Turn left along the road heading NE, then E, to Gatten Lodge and pass between the buildings before leaving the road, down to a pool on the right.

Take the gate on the right and traverse down the field alongside the pool to the far end. Go through a gate to turn right, skirting the pool on the right and going due E up a field to a gully. Passing a gate and with trees and rhododendrons on the left, go through a wooden gate, keeping right of the crest, and pass between a small pool and a fence on the left and Leasowes Bank Farm on the left. Cross a rail-and-wire stile and continue right, down a track, then follow it left down and up past Buzzard's Breg on the left, to a T-junction with the road. Turn left and, opposite New Leasowes Farm, turn right steeply up a green, hedged track to a stile and go left past gorse, then immediately right, steeply up (ESE) to reach a metal gate and tumulus up on the left.

Skirting around with the tumulus summit of Cothercott Hill on the left, continue ENE and gradually descend for approximately 600m over a field with a lone tree on the left to arrive at a stile between two trees. Cross onto the road with Thresholds on the right.

Go left (E) for approximately 100m and, opposite a Shropshire Way stile ③ on the left, go directly right through a waymarked gate onto the metalled grass and hedged track of The Port Way.

Continue gradually down on an undulating route (SE) with gorse to the right and hedges to the left. Arriving at a gate, cross into an open field, keeping to the metalled track with a wire fence on the right, past a stone building on the right to a further gate adjacent to a wooden building on the right.

Continue on the field track going left (ESE) with the hedge still on the right-hand side and Betchcott Hill trig point on the right in the next field. Follow the field down to a wide grass/gorse track (wire fence on the right) and head SE, then S, down to a gate, to proceed with the hedge/wire fence now on the left.

Walk up to a further gate and over the crest, continuing straight on at the next gate (not turning left) with Hawkham Hollow on the left. Now heading on a SE bearing with a fence on the left, continue to a sheep dip with double gates and a pool on the left. Walk past a fir/beech wood on the left to a gate and drop down to the dip at the end of High Park Hollow, then go left (E) up a track to join a further metalled track 4.

Cross diagonally over at a cattle grid and continue on the same bearing with a hedge/fence on the left. You will now leave The Port Way as you reach the National Trust property of the Long Mynd. Follow a grass track gradually down ENE and, at a marker on the right, go right along a grass track heading E, over Cross Dyke. With Jonathan's Hollow down on the right join the Picklescott–All Stretton road just above Jinlye and Worsley 5. Continue SW steeply down into All Stretton village – roughly 1km.

Section 40
All Stretton to Cressage

Distance:	21.3km (13¼ miles)
Grade:	Moderate
Terrain:	Quiet lanes, steep footpaths over hills, bridleways and tracks over farmland and wooded areas
Maps:	OS Explorers 217: The Long Mynd and Wenlock Edge and 241: Shrewsbury
Route Map:	Map 28; Page 119
Guide Time:	7 hours

Depart from the Stretton Hall Hotel 1 turning left and, heading SSW. Take the first turn to the left into Farm Lane and continue into Starr Lane.

Continue straight on over the railway bridge past Long Mynd View to the main A49 road. Cross diagonally right to a stile. Enter a rising field with a hedge

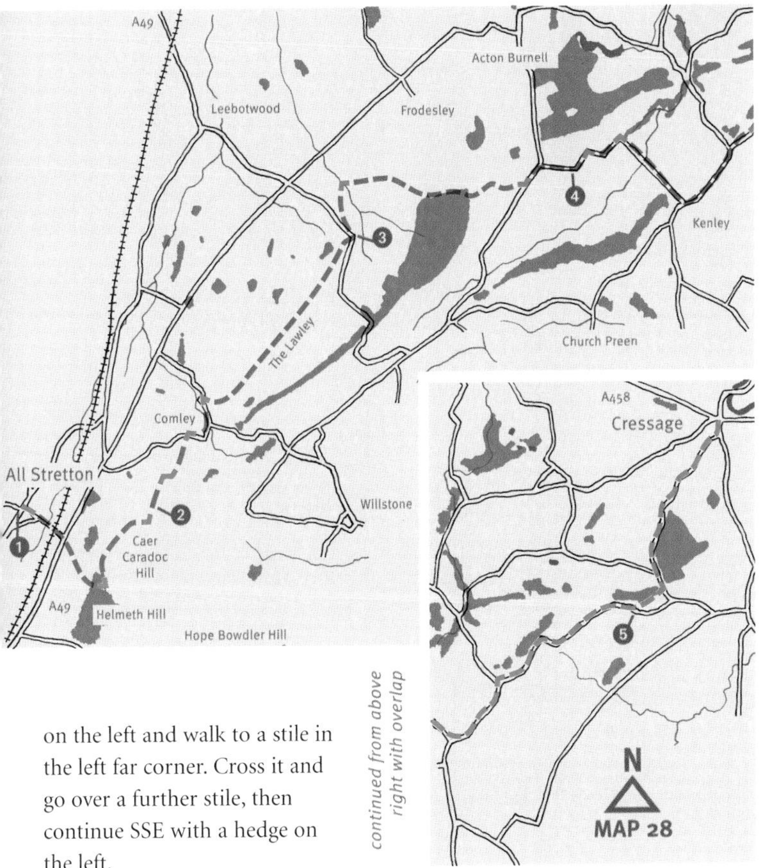

on the left and walk to a stile in the left far corner. Cross it and go over a further stile, then continue SSE with a hedge on the left.

You will now find a pool down on the right, adjacent to New House Farm. Take a stile on the left at the raised end of the field and skirt the wire fence on the right (heading SE) past two more pools on the right. Pass through a wooden gate on the same contour to arrive at a metal gate with a wooden stile.

Cross into an inclined wood area with a brook down on the right. Caer Caradoc rises steeply to the left (N). Your path joins the brook and then veers left past a footbridge on the right. Here search out a steeply rising track on the left, heading NNE and then NNW up to a stile. Cross the stile and proceed NNW (ignore the waymarks indicating left or right) up the steep path to Three Fingers Rock.

Continue on a NE heading over the spine of Caer Caradoc to the top ❷. Descend Caradoc on a NE bearing, picking up a wire fence on the right with the Lawley and the Wrekin straight ahead. Continue to descend to a stile waymarked Ippikin's Way with a gully to the right. Continue straight on down but gradually right into a dip with a white house ahead on the hill opposite, meeting with a stile in the right-hand corner of a field.

Cross into a small rough bracken-covered field and proceed NNE then NE to a further stile in a hedge and into the lane beyond. Cross over the lane and locate a footbridge over the stream. Cross it and a further stile into a field. Follow the hedge for a short distance and then walk away from it, heading NE, to a stream with a footbridge. Go over this and up to a stile in a hedge onto a lane.

Turn left down the lane towards Comley and, at a junction, turn right. There's a Georgian post box in the hedge on the right. Carefully look for a right turn along the lane up a track past a white cottage. This track is waymarked and rises, veering right to a cattle grid. Cross this and immediately leave the track and continue up the bank on the right, rising to a gate.

Passing through the gate, ignore the main track on the right and carry straight on, steeply up the Lawley on a ENE bearing with Shoot Rough on the right. Continue climbing on the spine past an old settlement area. Walk to the end then head down through a beautiful wooded glade to a stile leading down to a lane ❸.

Turn left down the lane, go round a sharp bend, taking care to locate a double gate at a further bend, on your right (no waymark). Go through the gate into a field heading N, diagonally across the field to the opposite left corner. Take the left of two gates and proceed with a hedge on the right veering right with Bentley Ford Farm on the right.
At the end of the field, pass through a gate to a hardcore track, turn right and walk

through a farmyard past Home Farm House and turn left through a gate. Continue E along a rising track to Park Farm with Lodge Hill and Causeway Wood ahead right on the skyline. Pass through a gate to a T-junction in the track. Cross directly opposite, through a gate, and through the next three fields on an ESE bearing. In the fourth field, wheel left at an electricity pole along a grass track bearing ENE towards Frodesley Lodge.

Turn right after passing through a gate at the top left corner and continue up the track into Lodge Hill Wood. Go through a gate to join a forest track, turning left, with the Lodge down on the left. The track skirts Lodge Hill Wood and, on a rise, the main track bears right. You should proceed straight here, down a lesser track with a derelict stone cottage on the right.

Pass through a gate onto a grass track with a hedge on the right and continue E over a narrowing field, ignoring the track going down on the left. The wire fence converges with the hedge at the end of the field with a waymarked gate. Pass through onto a deviating hedged track and emerge onto a lane at a T-junction with West Farm on the left, constructed of red brick, and Stonehouse Farm opposite. Turn left along a low walled lane passing a stone cottage on the right and pass between the buildings of Ruckley Hall Farm. Turn right at the junction for Langley Chapel, opposite Laurel Cottage, to go down a hedged lane veering left, with Langley Hall to the ENE straight ahead. Pass a chapel in a field on the right ❹. This is the stone built Langley Chapel with its open wooden bell tower.

Go past Langley Hall and farm on the right and cross two white-railed bridges over streams with Langley Cottage on the right. Continue along the lane heading NE with the Wrekin ahead and a stream in a tree-lined gully on the left. Shortly, turn right along the lane on a SE heading and continue to the top of the ridge to a T-junction, in the hamlet of Parkgate. Follow the signpost to Acton Burnell and Harley. Continue along the lane passing Rose Cottage on your left and into a dip with a picturesque thatched stone cottage on the right (Bank Cottage). Go straight on over the T-junction and pass Church Farm buildings on both the left and the right. Carry on past the timbered/stone Keld Cottage on the right.

Further on, at a bend to the left, with the road veering right, is St John's Church. Beyond, on the right, are the Old School House and the Old Rectory – built with a mix of stone and red brick, slate and tile.

Continue along the lane, leaving Kenley with its wonderful view over Wenlock Edge to the S. The lane passes Broomcroft and Little Broomcroft on the left. Continue along the lane, skirting Lord's Coppice on the left. At a right-hand bend ❺, go left off the lane just before a building on the left. Pass a gate on an ENE heading and, just inside the edge of the coppice, head down a deviating steep path to double wooden gates onto Wood Lane. This is a permissive path, used by kind permission of the Raby Estate. It is not a public right of way.

Proceeding N, down past Park Coppice and Tudor's Plantation on the right. The lane drops down with the Wrekin and a church ahead. Enter Cressage at a T-junction with the A458.

Caer Caradoc and the Lawley

Section 41
Cressage to Wellington

Distance:	11.7km (7¼ miles)
Grade:	Easy/moderate
Terrain:	Metalled roads, tracks and footpaths including steep ascent of the Wrekin
Maps:	OS Explorers 241: Shrewsbury and 242: Telford, Ironbridge and the Wrekin
Route Map:	Map 29; Page 124
Guide Time:	3 hours

From the war memorial ❶ in the centre of the village, branch off right, into the road signposted B4380 to Telford. Continue along the road to reach a stone bridge over the River Severn.

Leave the road just after the bridge, going right and down into a field with two fir trees on the left and the river on the right. Cross a gate and keep the river on your right, following the hedge to large willow trees and through a further gate. After 50m, at a single oak tree, head left bearing NE, following fenced woodland on the left.

At the crest of the rise, and after the wood, leave the fence while continuing on the same bearing, straight past a fir tree and down a track with a sunken stream. With a line of trees on the right, proceed up through a kissing gate to the main road in the village of Leighton, joining the B4380 ❷.

Cross the road and turn left past the Kynnersley Arms on the left, then proceed right, up School Lane heading ENE. Continue on the lane, which bears left (N) and down to the mill (Dingle Mill), then go up the rise heading NE for approximately 750m to reach a sharp left-hand bend in the lane. At this bend, leave the lane and go ahead into the field on the same bearing. Cross the stile on the far side of the field to join Spout Lane ❸. Turn right heading towards Little Wenlock. At the scout camp on your left, turn left to go through the camp on a rising track. Pass through Gibbons Coppice (N) up to the circuit base track of the Wrekin. Continue right (NE), then shortly turn left, steeply up (NW), by a small cairn, to the Raven's Bowl, keeping right of the rocky outcrop to the trig point and the summit of the Wrekin ❹. Follow the main footpath to the right (NE) down to the gate at the bottom, via Wrekin Cottage. When you reach the metalled road bear left and continue under the M54 bridge ❺ following the main road for a further 700m to reach the Falcon Hotel on the corner of Haygate Road. Turn left into Haygate Road and continue to the end of the road, crossing the Ring Road into Walker Street and Wellington Town Square.

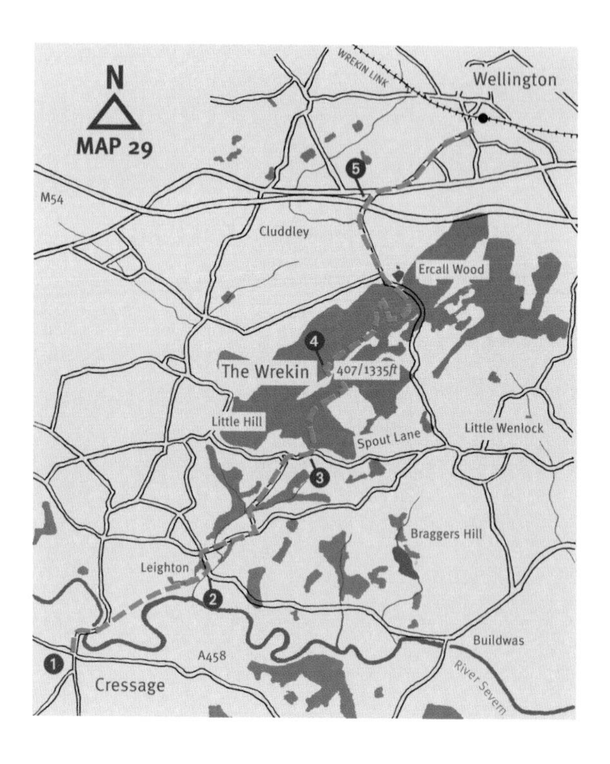

Congratulations – you have now been 'All around the Wrekin'!

Back on the Wrekin

Acknowledgements

There is a small number of people who have made a significant contribution to the creation of this book to whom we are especially grateful.

First and foremost to those members and former members of Wrekin Rotary Club who have put so much time, energy and effort into every dimension of the whole project.

A special debt of gratitude to Sir Chris Bonington for the Foreword.

Chris Bagshaw and Lucy Berrett at Outcrop Publishing Services for all their help and advice, and for converting our efforts into the completed guide book. Mark Richards for his well illustrated maps and infectious enthusiasm.

As well as our Principal Sponsors, there have been a considerable number of smaller donations from every section of the community for which we are very grateful.

Special thanks to the proof readers and others who have made a contribution directly or indirectly to the production of this guidebook.

Thanks also for the assistance of several landowners that have allowed us to use permissive paths across their land.

Stuart Mackintosh, Countryside Services Manager at Powys County Council for help and advice in so many areas.

To all the rights of way officers at all the local authorities for their guidance and support.

Finally, a heartfelt thank you to the wives, partners and families of the Wrekin Rotarian Walkers, for all their love, encouragement and understanding, particularly through all the difficult times and extended trips. A great many miles were walked in preparing this book so apologies for not always being around when perhaps we should have been.

The Countryside Code

• Be safe – plan ahead and follow any signs

Even when going out locally, it's best to get the latest information about where and when you can go; for example, your rights to go onto some areas of open land may be restricted while work is carried out, for safety reasons or during breeding seasons. Follow advice and local signs, and be prepared for the unexpected.

• Leave gates and property as you find them

Please respect the working life of the countryside, as our actions can affect people's livelihoods, our heritage, and the safety and welfare of animals and ourselves.

• Protect plants and animals, and take your litter home

We have a responsibility to protect our countryside now and for future generations, so make sure you don't harm animals, birds, plants, or trees.

• Keep dogs under close control

The countryside is a great place to exercise dogs, but it's every owner's duty to make sure their dog is not a danger or nuisance to farm animals, wildlife or other people.

• Consider other people

Showing consideration and respect for other people makes the countryside a pleasant environment for everyone – at home, at work and at leisure.

Picture Credits

All the pictures used in this book were taken by Ken Wagstaffe, except p11 and back cover, bottom right (Graham Leddington) and p109 and back cover, top left (Jim Needham).

Principal Sponsors

It has taken five years of dedication, hard work and sheer determination by a group of enthusiastic people, mainly from Wrekin Rotary Club, to bring this ambitious project towards a successful conclusion. The other key element needed to complete the venture was financial support. Whilst a worthwhile amount was raised through well-supported concerts and other events, the majority needed to be raised elsewhere. This was crucial to ensure that Hope House Children's Respite Hospice could benefit by the maximum amount possible from the sale of this guide book.

Without the overwhelming generosity of our principal sponsors this publication would not have been possible. We are extremely grateful for their encouragement, faith and substantial contributions.

ELLIOTT BRIDGMAN
SOLICITORS

Alan and Margaret Leddington

B J Ward (Farms)